TORAH BRIGHT

It Takes Courage

TORAH BRIGHT

It Takes Courage

NEW
HOLLAND

'You will never do anything in this world without courage.
It is the greatest quality of mind next to honour.'
– Aristotle

ACKNOWLEDGEMENTS

So many people have helped me reach where I am today. I have experienced an extraordinary amount of kindness from friends and strangers alike. I have tried to mention as many of you as possible. I know I would not have this story to tell without you. Sending infinite love and gratitude to you all – you know who you are.

This book is dedicated to my family who have shaped my life in profound ways and have set me on the path to becoming all I can be.

To my mother, Marion, who is ahead of her time, who imparted the joy of seeking knowledge, who showed me how to be a mother and who is always teaching me how to love and live wisely. *Sorella Bella.*

To my father, Peter, who taught me both how to work hard and the value of sacrifice. Who built block towers in the wee hours of the night with me when I couldn't sleep as a child and who imparted his love of fast cars.

To my brother, Robin, the first snowboarder of us all – who showed me how to triumph over adversity and taught me that, if we take charge, our personal evolution can be constant and continuous.

To my sister, Rowena, my partner in late night laughs, who taught me how to find beauty, how to live on purpose, and how to make things happen. *Sorella Bella.*

To my brother, Ben, my mentor, my coach, my friend, who taught me the power of the mind and body, who gave me permission to soar, to think outside the box and to never conform.

To my sister Abi, who showed me how to bring the fun, how to be loyal, how to live passionately and how to forget about what others think of me. *Sorella Bella*.

To my nieces and nephews: Janaya, Isabella, Syd, Lyon, Thor and Oliver. Thank you for loving me so purely. Thank you for giving me a clearer view of the mysteries, realities and joys of my potential here on earth. Thank you for allowing me to be your Aunty Mummy.

To my cousin Sophia, for getting into my head, writing her way through long days, and making this book happen. Forever grateful. *Sorella Bella*.

Torah xo

CONTENTS

Preface, Circe Wallace   11

Introduction   17

Run One   21

Run Two   32

Run Three   41

Run Four   46

Run Five   53

Run Six   63

Run Seven   76

Run Eight   83

Run Nine   91

Run Ten   97

Run Eleven   109

Run Twelve   114

Run Thirteen   119

Run Fourteen   122

Run Fifteen   131

Run Sixteen   142

Run Seventeen   150

References   153

PREFACE

I woke up face down on the bed in a scarlet-red, one-piece ski suit of my own design. Gold glitter was everywhere, in my eyes, in my hair, in my nose. Big, chunky, glitter, clogging my view of my room, I even had gold boogers up my nose. It took me a minute to remember why I was there, asleep in my favorite cute hotel room at The Opus Hotel in the trendy area of Vancouver's Yaletown. The room was booked at the last minute. I still didn't know how I got so lucky, only calling a week before my arrival.

My own snowboarding career was successful, but short. Plagued by knee injuries, I knew I didn't have it in me anymore. When I was afraid to jump, or I couldn't keep up with the boys, I had to let it go. It was scary to start something new, something unknown. There was no college to learn about it, but I had been influential in creating a new business dedicated to representing and managing surfing, skating and snowboarding athletes. I had worked with athletes in the ski and snowboarding field for 13 years.

These activities I loved deeply. I had been a troubled kid in my teens, growing up in Northwest USA. I was into punk music, drugs and skateboarding. But it was to be snowboarding that would change my life and teach me everything I know. It was a whole new world.

So here I was, now aged 38, bathed in glitter, lying facedown in a hotel room. I shook the glitter off. I was still reeling from the night before. I am the agent for Torah Bright, the Olympic Gold medallist for the 2010 Women's Half Pipe. Everyone knew Torah had it in her, but it still was sinking in that she had got the gold.

Torah walked into my life at the tender age of 15, the same age that I had discovered snowboarding. I had been working with a couple of Australians and they encouraged me to look at this emerging talent from their homeland. I wasn't convinced. Let's face it, Australia isn't known for its mountains and snow athletes, and I was very selective about the women I would represent. My experience also taught me to watch out for young girls who often had little understanding of what it was like to travel alone or how to be challenged if they needed to be independently driven. Torah came to the US alone for the first time, funded by her hard-working parents. They knew she had something special, just like they knew her incredibly talented sister Rowena knew how to ski race. They knew Torah deserved a chance.

It wasn't until I met her face to face that I knew she was truly a phenomenon. She carries a sweetness that in most people I would take an aversion to. I am not one for sweet and innocent and it typically doesn't bode well for athletes who need to lurch themselves off cliffs, or into 22-foot half pipes. But there was something else, a fierceness, behind those sparkly eyes and amazing smile. I fell in love with her instantly.

I had been vocal about my opposition to snowboarding's inclusion in the Olympic Games. There is much history about snowboarding and its growth into a competitive sport that only the early adapters or insiders fully understand. At the time of its inclusion in the Nagano Olympic Games in Japan in 1998 the FIS (Fédération Internationale De Ski) had historically been opposed to snowboarders. We were called 'knuckle draggers' and had been given a mascot (the first ever mascot) in the form of 'Animal, the Muppet'. Yet somehow the FIS had won the bid to be our governing body, even though we already had our own organization for years, the ISF (International Snowboard Federation). Although controversial, in it's own right, it was the proper snowboarders' organization, but it lost the bid. Typical politics for the IOC (International Olympic Committee).

Conceptually, I loved the idea of competing for my country in the oldest and most respected sporting event in the world, the Olympic Games, but snowboarding was never just a sport to me. The reality that a ski federation would be governing our art form was blasphemy. Yet there was always a part of me that wondered what it would be like to be on that world stage.

Torah and I immediately established a lovely working relationship. She wouldn't make unreasonable demands; her mum, Marion, was intense but passionate and supportive, and I grew to love them both like family. We separated once as I moved agencies and I had to do some of my own growth and exploration to be my best self, but somehow, just prior to the Vancouver games, we ended up together again, and all was right in the world. Torah had trained unbelievably hard and, while her brother Benny and her had an up and down relationship, he was influential in bringing us back together again. For that I will always be grateful, as working with Torah has been a joy.

Watching Torah win her gold medal was intense. The Roxy girls and Danielle Beck, the Roxy brand manager at the time, had put considerable effort into supporting Torah onsite and on the day of the games. I sat with a group of girls, all snowboarders, who had been on the journey with her. They all carried jars of gold glitter. I had ridden for the Roxy team myself, as their first American girl snowboarder, so it felt like watching family with family.

Torah had hit her head numerous times going into Vancouver and there was a constant air of concern around her. She fell on her first run and it was anyone's game. We sat there tense, knowing she had it in her, but also knowing if she didn't land a clean run and complete her switch backside 720, we would all be going home deflated, being emotionally invested in our fragile but fierce friend.

She did it. We screamed and jumped for joy – in awe of her grace and beauty. No other woman rides like Torah. She is feminine, yet rides with strong determination and does tricks the other girls can't or won't do. She put it all on the line until the very end and she won. The rest of the evening was dedicated to press, dope testing and more press. There was no time for celebration. Gold medals come with a heavy burden of responsibility, to the Australian Olympic Committee, to the media and even to her own relationships. But the next night we had a huge party, and the glitter went everywhere!

Four years later, Torah would amaze me (and her fans) even more. She decided to do something no other athlete in snowboarding has or probably ever will do – compete in three events in Sochi, Russia. When she first shared this plan with me, I was floored. She had just lost her best friend in a traumatic injury while riding with her just a year prior; she had divorced her husband, and here she was pushing through despite the sorrow and heartbreak. I have worked with many unbelievably talented athletes but this was unprecedented.

There have been many long phone calls between us – I have lived longer, and I too have had my own heartbreak and injuries and have lost friends. It has been one of my greatest experiences being able to support this amazing woman and friend and be there on her ride. We have

PREFACE

cried together and I have been able to take some of the painful lessons I have learned the hard way and share in a life experience with a woman I admire and respect beyond words.

This girl continues to push through, advance snowboarding for her country and for women. She continues to amaze me with her strong determination, her ability to stay soft, and maintain an open heart. She is one of a kind.

Circe Wallace

Senior Vice-President

Action Sports Wasserman Media Group

INTRODUCTION

'Nothing splendid has ever been achieved except by those who dared believe that something inside of them was superior to circumstance.'
– Bruce Barton

On the outside my life resembled a fairy tale. I had an Olympic gold medal, the world was my playground and everything I could ever want was at my fingertips. On the inside I was broken. The life force that was once so strong inside me had steadily been drained away. I was barely functioning and all the while, I papered up the cracks with that 'Bright' smile I'm known for. Hoping no one would notice. I was fighting; fighting for the one thing I thought I cared most about, my marriage.

In 2012, on a typical November day with shining bluebird skies and crisp fresh snow in the mountains of Park City, Utah, I was no longer fighting. I was with my great friend and snowboarder, Scotty James. There was a shift. I was different. For the first time in years I was having the best time snowboarding. I felt free and balanced. I felt like my snowboard was a part of me. This was a sensation I hadn't experienced since the inner turmoil began. I did not arrive at these feelings by chance. I'd made a choice.

It had been the hardest decision of my life to press for a divorce from my husband. My choice had caused a lot of pain. However, for what felt like the first time in years, I had put myself first. I chose life. I chose not to give up on the possibility of being truly loved. This was the first choice of many that I would make that would lead me to where I am now: alive and happy.

On that day in Park City, the 2012–13 northern winter was already underway. This was the Olympic qualifying year. I had no time to waste. I had a renewed love for both my snowboarding and for life. Snowboarding was my medicine. I was loving snowboarding the most I had since I was a 12-year-old kid. It was rejuvenating to be on the mountain and away from my thoughts and all the legal issues surrounding my pending divorce.

I spent a lot of time brain storming with Ben about how I could best get through this trying personal time and get myself back to where I needed to be on my snowboard. Our first plan was for me to 'just snowboard', to shred to the beat of my heart. Taking on three Olympic events was the winning idea. Ben had put this to me back in 2011 and I had laughed at him. Yet here we were, one year out from the Olympic Games, and I had committed to a task that many thought both ridiculous and impossible. For me, this decision was never about the chance of winning three Olympic gold medals. It was all about snowboarding and about sharing this magical sport with the world.

This book is a direct result of this period in my life. If there is one thing that I am most proud of, it is that I had the courage to choose *me* and my happiness. I was reading Stephanie Dowrick's *Forgiveness and Other Acts of Love* recently and her words made me realize that courage pushed me to survive the daily navigations between the known and the unknown. Courage helped me to deal with the inevitable. Courage allowed me to distinguish between what I could change and what I could not. Courage sustained me as I journeyed deep into my own particular version of hell.

INTRODUCTION

Courage gave me the strength and the grace to re-emerge, and still find life worth living.

I have won many titles and travelled to the most extraordinary places in the world. Sport has brought me skills and taught me life lessons I will never forget. However, looking back I realize that it is not the extraordinary aspects of my life that are beautiful to me. It is the wonder and marvel in the ordinary aspects of this life. It is the simple things that I love and am truly proud of. It is the joy I experience in laughing, the skills I am able to share with others including my sweet growing nephews and nieces. It is the friend, daughter, sister and aunt I am to those in my life. I write this with my newest nephew Oliver, a few days old, lying on my chest. I can't help but stop, look at and kiss his sweet face. These are my life's true joys.

I wanted to write the story of my journey to help others find the courage to see them through their adversity and to believe in themselves even in their darkest moments. For as Oz tells the (not-so-cowardly) lion in L. Frank Baum's *The Wonderful World of Oz* '[a]ll you need is confidence in yourself. There is no living thing that is not afraid when it faces danger. The true courage is in facing danger when you are afraid.'

This book is also for my family – the future generation. My growing nieces and nephews, my future children and all the children of the world. May they see the joy and adventures that come from finding your passion and living on purpose, from working hard, by living wholeheartedly, with courage.

RUN ONE

'One sees clearly only with the heart. Anything essential is invisible to the eyes.'

– Antoine De Saint-Exupéry

I have chased snow around in circles around the world, up the Utah and Colorado Mountains, down the Sierra Nevadas, in and out of the Canadian Rockies, through European Alps, across the snow-capped peaks of Japan, New Zealand, and South America. Riding and shredding in alpine regions all over the world has defined my life since the day I turned 14. My relationship with the snow was born long before, but that year, I began travelling my inverted journey of the birds of migration. From that day onwards, every year, I would fly north for the winter and south for the winter, dividing my time between Utah and the southern snowfields of Australia. Endless winter might sound like a curse placed on Narnia, but for me, it's been a blessing and a (hard won) dream.

It is funny how things turn out. In a very possible parallel universe I could have grown up a city girl, surfing the waves of the Pacific Ocean, instead of the snow-packed walls of a half pipe. My mum, Marion Davidson, and dad, Peter Bright, were both born and raised on Sydney's North Shore. Mum and dad loved the Northern Beaches of Sydney when they were growing up, and have transferred that love to me. The unique combination of orange sand, green Norfolk Island Pines, and deep blue water that can be found on that stretch of coast is nothing short of enchanting, and I relish the opportunity to surf there when I'm in Sydney. I love the ocean and all of its wonders. It is a majestic, powerful and calming force. Despite my busy snow schedule, and unerring commitment to the slopes I still make time for the sea. My annual surfing safaris to Hawaii, Costa Rica or Nicaragua are some of the most important dates in my dairy.

Fate intervened, and instead of growing up on the North Shore as my parents had, I grew up in the shadow of Australia's stunning alpine region in a little town called Cooma. Situated just one and a half hours from Cooma are the snowfields, the Pacific Coast and the nation's capital; Canberra. The Kosciuszko National Park surrounds Australia's highest peak, Mt Kosciuszko. While not high by world standards, we have vast rolling areas of snow and peaks. Cooma is the largest town in the region and is the place (despite being technically a nomad) I call home. A road sign as you enter the town announces that Cooma is the 'gateway to the Snowy Mountains'. It is through, and thanks to this 'gateway' that I found my path, and never looked back.

When Peter was younger, he loved to escape from Sydney to his mother's families' property at Numeralla near Cooma and so, after leaving school he moved there to work the land with them. Mum and dad had friends in common and had noticed each other at various Sydney parties however it took Cooma to bring them together. Peter's sister, Marie Hampson (née Bright) who was working as a nurse in Cooma at the time invited some mutual friends to attend the Bungarby Buck's Party, put on by a group of young adults in the Cooma region. Marion tagged along for the trip and Peter put them up for the weekend at Numeralla. Mum was due to travel to

Melbourne on holidays several weeks later, and dad coyly suggested she could break up the drive by stopping over to visit him at Numeralla if she wanted. She did, and, well, she never made it to Melbourne.

Mum made herself useful around the farm; she mustered cattle, loaded hay bales and managed to be thrown off a horse three times while dad taught her to ride. Dad also taught mum how to shoot a rifle and how to catch trout fresh from the river for breakfast. Marion was in her element on that working-date-holiday, she adored the Monaro country and the satisfaction of working outdoors; connected to the land. It seemed you could take the girl out of the city *and* vice versa. A long-distance courtship ensued and many more trips up and down the Hume Highway from Sydney were made over the succeeding year. Mum eventually moved to Canberra for her postgraduate midwifery study in order to be closer to dad. Their friendship blossomed into a deep love and they were married in a romantic, rustic old stone Catholic Church at Hunter's Hill in Sydney on April 12, 1973.

Dad was a keen skier so the first winter they were married he took mum skiing at Thredbo and she was instantly hooked. From then on, they skied at least two days of every week. Mum was a water-baby in Sydney but says she found herself a new home in the mountains and on the snow. She has always said that she finds the sheer beauty, peace and rhythms of the Snowies completely inspiring. Our love of the alpine wilderness is definitely deep in our blood.

My eldest brother and sister, Robin and Rowena, were born in 1978 and 1980. They all lived at Numeralla until Robin was four and they moved to their own property on Wambrook Hill on the Snowy Mountains Highway, 20 minutes out of Cooma on the way to Adaminaby. It was in a sheep grazing area and they named the property, Colby. Colby was my first home, as well the place where my brother Benjamin, my sister Abish, and I were born. Ben in 1984, I followed in 1986 and Abi arrived in 1989. Mum says she always wanted to have a large family. She and her older sister Jill had been inseparable, but tragically, Jill had died when they were both very young. Shortly after Jill's death her younger brother Richard was born and she also loved him dearly as they were growing up. She wanted us to be able to enjoy and support each other as they had done.

Life on the farm was healthy and busy, ideal for a family of five kids. We breathed fresh country air, drank crystal clear spring water and our little home was full of love. The first stage of our house was made from a 'kit home' that dad assembled with some help from family and friends. It was ecologically designed, and built facing north on a large plateau on the highest part of our property. In the winter it had a sensational fog drenched view of the valley below through stands of elegant tall gum trees. We were 1150 meters above sea level but the climate felt temperate; the summers were soft and there was always a gentle breeze. In the winter, the sun would stream in, heating up the black slate floors where we would play for hours on end. A pergola that extended the length of our north facing, floor-to-ceiling glass walls filtered the sun. Stone was collected from the farm to build the two exterior walls, which created both a rustic look and functioned as heat banks.

All of the Bright children were on skis as soon as we could stand up. Snow fell regularly on our property and I loved watching Rob and Rowe carve through the landscape on their cross-country skis while Ben would shuffle around on little plastic skis behind them. We all enjoyed our days on the cross-country trails at Cabramurra during winter. One of the little ones (Abi or I) would sit in a backpack and the other would be pulled along behind in a sled while the three older children raced ahead on their skis, exploring the magical trails. I won my first trophy on cross-country skis at Cabramurra on a round track for under fives. As members of the Cabramurra Ski Club, we learned to downhill ski and participated in the Tuesday night races that the older Bright kids raced in. While the others could get on the one poma lift (a circular disc that goes between your legs to pull you up the slope), mum would take me up via a rope tow and ski me down a gentle slope between her legs, sometimes with Abi on her back. One of the reasons mum had us involved in outdoors activities was that she believed it promoted peaceful living. She was right. A transformation occurred when we were outside on our adventures. I felt strong and confident and free.

Summers on the farm were equally fun. Dad set up rope swings from the trees, a climbing frame and a big sand pit. We also had a motorbike, push bikes and two horses. Mum played tennis with us on a makeshift court (a flat dirt road at the back of the house). While we played, we loved watching dad and the dogs work in the sheep yards and shearing shed. Lake Eucumbene was just a 10-minute drive, and mum, who had been a competitive swimmer when she was younger, taught my older siblings to swim there. We also enjoyed hiking to a stunning waterfall on the boundary of the property for picnics when friends came by. The place teamed with wildlife too. There was a family of kangaroos I adored who would visit our front yard early every day to wish us good morning.

We had goats for milking, including a mad buck that ate all our clothes off the washing line and snacked on our western red cedar windows. We loved him despite his destructive dietary habits, however the thought of continually replacing our clothes (and of unwanted window extensions) forced dad to give him away. Dad was an animal whisperer. He kept a pet blue tongue lizard and always fed the native birds. Not all Australian wildlife is pleasant though. One of my strongest memories of that time was of playing in the bush with my older siblings and watching Ben and Rowe riding off on their bikes, leaving me calling after them. I was so frustrated; I wanted to be on a bike too. Little did I know that was the least of my worries, I was smack in the middle of an ant's nest. I remember being very sore and swollen for days.

When mum and dad decided to start a family, they became focused on learning how to live a healthy life in order to give their children the best start possible. Marion developed an avid interest in natural health, energy medicine, and alternative therapies. Nowadays the wonders of quantum physics, modern alternative health technology and future medicine in the world of epigenetics excite her study and practice. I used to think the food our family ate was strange. I now realize that we were just proto-hipsters. We were downing green smoothies and eating kale-chia-quinoa-mush 25 years before it was cool. Which, by hipster-logic, means we were *really* cool. Cooma didn't see it that way. Kids at my primary school used to call mum a witch. Mum just wanted us to be strong and resilient. I remember mum had this metaphor about cars, she would ask us: "Would you put sugar into a Porsche engine? No, you'd put premium grade petrol in it because it's a finely tuned race car." I'm still not really sure I want to think of my body as a car, but I understood what she meant. We need to be considered about what we put into our bodies so we can function at our best. I still like the odd sugar hit though.

I didn't mind that people thought we were weird. I knew mum was definitely a good witch. She was always fixing me up when I was sick or had an injury. She used all sorts of interesting natural remedies, and practiced energy healing with crystals. When I was very little my favorite toy was my 'wee doll'. I loved her. As you can probably guess, 'wee doll' was named as such because you could fill her up with water, and then she would wee where you aimed her. Unfortunately, I was too small to reach the tap on my own and had to ask my older siblings to fill her up for me. They weren't always obliging. I was impatient one afternoon and so I climbed up onto the bathtub so that I could lean over to reach the basin. I slipped and smashed open my chin. Mum used steri-strips to close it up and then used her crystal torch with colour therapy additions to promote healing. To her satisfaction I would have been scar-less but several weeks later, I tripped over, slamming my chin on a gutter and splitting it open again. Mum just patched it up again and we kept on going. She was a useful witch to have around.

Spiritual health was as important to her as physical health, and she had many unanswered questions on mystical matters. Both my parents were brought up in 'good Catholic families', but for a number of years had not been practicing. As she was embarking on the adventure of raising children, she became concerned about finding something she believed would offer her family strong guidance and principles. She set out to investigate all realms of spiritual belief and non-belief. She studied atheism, agnosticism, Judaism, Islam, Buddhism, and the Hare Krishnas. She loved many aspects of all these faiths and philosophies but still hadn't found a spirituality she wanted to teach her children. None answered her questions to her satisfaction.

Bill and Heather Davison, a couple that mum had had some business dealings with, wanted to give their children the 'snow experience'. Mum and dad loved hosting and so invited them to stay with us during the holidays. They were very involved members of The Church Of Jesus Christ Of Latter-day Saints, (Mormons by nickname). Mum had not yet encountered this religion and she was ignited and inspired by their introduction. She asked lots of questions and when they left she continued to study. She read the philosophical and intellectual works of many Latter-day scholars. Months later, Peter, Marion, Robin and Rowe became part of the small chapter of the church in Cooma, joining six other families.

One of the books that Marion most loved was called *The Ways and Power of Love* by C. Kay Allen. Mum was very taken by the central concept that 'God has not given us the spirit of fear; but of power and of love.' She strongly believes that there are three modes, or frequencies that we can live and operate within. We can decide whether to have love and trust as our motivating force, or run on either a duty/justice or a fear/anxiety level. What always resonated with me was the idea that we could choose to live in a world of love/trust energy. Mum believes that the desire to love and be loved is universal. Her intention was to instill in us the courage to magnify our talents and live purposely in our world, whilst seeing unconditional love as the creative energy and central governing concept of life. Love is the cement that holds us together even when personal storms rage. Living this, at times, has proved to be harder than she expected. Life has thrown many challenging lessons at each of the Brights on our individual and collective journeys.

We all enjoyed life on our farm, but unfortunately it was a very tough time for my parents. I didn't understand this until much later, but an extreme drought had cast its dry breath over the Monaro. Mum and dad had innovative ideas for permaculture farming using Rudolf Steiner's advanced agricultural methods, but they needed a good rainfall to execute them, which we weren't getting. Because of the drought, our sheep had to be hand-fed with expensive purchased fodder. As well as operating the farm, dad was forced to find extra work to make ends meet. To make matters worse, interest rates were rising to outlandish levels. The farm was eventually divided up and sold. Our neighbours, the Coles, purchased the good grazing land. We remained friends with the family and their eldest son Tom and I became good friends at high school and remain so.

In 1989 we officially became known as the 'Cooma Brights'. We moved down the hill and into a new chapter of our lives. It was a big change that took more than a little adjustment. The good news was that mum didn't have to drive in and out of town with all of us so often for our various music lessons, swimming squads, scouts meetings, and soccer practice sessions. No longer having acres to roam around in was a big loss and we were all a little stir-crazy. Ben in particular hated being in a confined yard and kept finding a way out. We were always looking for him. One night it was getting quite late and we hadn't seen him for hours. Dad was out of town working so we had to ask friends to help us search. Mum was quietly frantic and so she decided to stop and pray in the house. That's when she found him curled up asleep under a mini trampoline exercizer in the corner of the lounge room.

Ben was soon to commence school at Cooma North Public with Rob and Rowe. That transition helped as he enjoyed the long walk to school with other kids. Rowe loved the move as she was great friends with Penny Carroll, whose family lived just up from us on the edge of Cooma North Nature Reserve. She could now spend much more time with her friend. Dad, meanwhile, had been doing a lot of work with farmers and their water supplies during the drought. He had worked with irrigation and pumping on the river flats at Numeralla. He was putting his many skills in that field to work for others. He retrained and established his business specialising in innovative pumping, water supply and irrigation, mostly for farming situations but also for housing subdivisions and for a local racecourse.

Cooma is not a typical Australian country town. It became a mecca of multiculturalism in the 1950s and 1960s when a massive engineering project commenced, the Snowy Mountains Hydro Electricity Scheme.

RUN ONE

To help agricultural production and feed the energy needs of the booming cities, the Australian government embarked on this enormous project. The scheme captured worldwide attention as something like this had never attempted on such a large scale. Multiple dams, power stations and underground tunnels diverted the snow-fed waters of the great Snowy River inland for irrigation and, at the same time, used the falling water to create hydroelectricity. My grandfather's two brothers were involved with this scheme; one as an engineer who worked from Adaminaby, a small town in the Monaro district, the other worked with the Department of Water Conservation and Irrigation. Thousands of immigrants came to Cooma and the region of the Snowies to work on the scheme. The labourers were mainly from Europe and Scandinavia, however, with Utah Constructions involved, many Americans came to take part. Interestingly, the Cooma branch of the church that had become such an integral part of our lives came to fruition in the days of the Snowy Mountains Hydro Electricity Scheme. American church members were among those who came to Australia on assignment and to work on the construction. Cooma swelled as it became the base for both the management team and for those who were on rest and recreation leave from the construction sites. The scheme brought creativity and courage to our area. Sadly the work was dangerous and many workers died during the construction.

Cooma afforded us a magical childhood. We certainly had our struggles under the conditions, but our devoted parents selflessly shouldered those burdens. They worked incredibly hard so we could have everything we needed and many of the things we wanted. We would never have been as free nor have been able to enjoy such a variety of experiences if we hadn't found our gateway to the Snowy Mountains. There are many generous, kind, creative, courageous and loving people in Cooma and its surrounding areas. I am so grateful for the time I spent with these amazing people before my life changed forever, and I became largely an expat, living on the other side of the world.

RUN TWO

'We are what we repeatedly do. Excellence therefore is not an act but a habit.'
– Aristotle

I started school at Cooma North Public. Rowena and Robin had left by the time I started but it was nice to have my big brother Ben at school with me, and eventually Abi who started three years later. She was a warrior of a little kid who would gallantly protect the quieter children from the bullies. She was tough as nails from a very young age, and refused to suffer fools. In those days, she'd tell anyone who'd listen that she was going to be a truck driver *and* a ballerina when she grew up. I admired (and still do) her strength and rambunctious will. I loved learning and I found many activities that excited me. Mrs Cox taught me piano and our friends, Jane Carroll and Jenny Slatyer, taught me to play the flute. I also sang in the choir and was part of the rhythmic ribbon-dancing group. Although I had a range of interests and abilities, sport received most of my attention.

Going to a school at the base of the Snowy Mountains meant that all the students were given the option to participate in one day of skiing a week during the winter, which of course we took advantage of. On top of that, mum would often take us out of school for our own training.

We might have missed a bit of school for the snow, but frustratingly we were never allowed to miss church, no matter how good the powder was. Mum maintained that Sunday was 'the Lord's day'. After we had attended the service and classes we had to have a quiet day with our family. We weren't even allowed to bounce on the trampoline; mum was very strict about that. Sundays felt like another school day because of all the church classes we attended. I am grateful I am now my own person and can choose how to spend my Sundays. Nowadays I choose to immerse myself in my surroundings, or spend time with my friends and family, or read something that is inspiring and challenges my ideas. We all find our own ways to connect with those deeper parts of ourselves. I still attend church if I want to be uplifted in a particular way. However, the most important aspect of spirituality for me is to have a personal and communicative relationship with God, to live according to my conscience, and to likewise allow all others that right.

It quickly became clear that all the Bright kids were gifted at both winter and summer sports. We didn't discriminate and immersed ourselves in everything on offer. We played soccer, netball, and basketball; and trained in athletics, swimming, gymnastics, and cross-country running. We joined a number of the sports clubs in Cooma and competed in most of the school teams. We also got great results. I was particularly proud that I held the walking record for many years at the Cooma Little Athletics Club.

Dad taught us that if we were going to put our time or energy into something, we had to give it our all. "If you are going to bother doing something, you better give it your whole heart, 110% effort" dad would say. Then he'd add, "but always make sure you have lots of fun too." We were all aware that whenever we put a bit of time into any sport, we quickly became really good at it, and that the better we became, the more fun we could have. Mum wanted us to experience a variety of sports so we could make informed choices about what we wanted to pursue in the future. She saw cross training as an important part of making the right choices.

A strong work ethic is in our genes. My parents led by example. We could see that they put their whole heart, soul and resources into raising our family and making our lives great. It seemed natural that we should likewise put all of our heart into anything we did. Rowe and I realized just recently how deeply this runs in us when we endeavoured to make a perfect pavlova together. We were so anxious to get it right that we made 12 attempts, (we take sugar as seriously as we take snow) but we also laughed all day. The best trick I learned was how to embrace the capacity for fun. Fun, for me, is an integral part of hard work. This is something I learned before I could walk, from my favorite childhood film, *Mary Poppins*. The opening lines to Poppins' clean-up-the-nursery ditty have forever resonated with me. 'In every job that must be done, there is an element of fun. You find the fun, and – snap – the job's a game.' The song speaks to me about so much more than tidying my bedroom (though it helps me do that too). This quote balances me and gives me my edge. I always find the fun, and then every trick I undertake becomes a piece of cake (or pavlova). There is the serious side to what I do, I am expected to perform and my work is dangerous, however, to borrow the words of Oscar Wilde, 'life is far too important a thing to ever talk seriously about'. I know if I lose the joy in what I do then I've lost everything.

Rowena was just four years old when she decided she would be an Olympian. On a frosty winter morning she was cuddled up with mum watching the 1984 Summer Olympic Games on TV from Los Angeles, California. She remembers vividly when diver Greg Louganis, won double gold on springboard and platform. She also recalls when the Australian swimmer, Jon Sieben, won the 200m Butterfly as an underdog against the world record holder (whom the announcers called 'the Albatross'). Apparently mum got really excited when the Mormon gymnast, Peter Vidmar, won his gold and silver medals. However it was the tiny gymnast Mary Lou Retton, who lit the Olympic spirit in Rowe's 4-year-old heart. Mary Lou twisted, turned, balanced, jumped and flew into Olympic history with such poised form and skill. She mesmerized tiny-Rowe. Rowe announced to mum her ambition and set about making it happen almost immediately. Rowe trained for many years with Cooma Gymnastics, as did I. While neither of us became gymnasts, this training was very helpful for our snow careers.

From an early age Rowe achieved outstanding results. She blazed a trail for our family in the international sports arena. Rowena had incredible style, technique, stamina and power in both skiing and in her summer sports. She always made it to the state-level at the primary school cross-country running championships, and in school swimming. In her first year of competitive swimming in the 10-year-old division, she brought home a bronze from the Country Championships. She won gold in breaststroke in year six and seven and competed in triathlons at state level. In fitness testings, at 15 years of age, her maximum volume of oxygen used, or VO2 max, tested at 76. This score is equal to scores from professional endurance champions like marathon runners. The highest score ever recorded for a woman is 78. We think she got her lungs from dad. She was encouraged to take up some kind of endurance sport.

Rowena loved swimming and was lucky to have a really talented swimming coach in Cooma. Rowe was very driven. During the summer holidays she would walk down to the local Cooma pool at 6 am for two hours of swimming training. She would return at noon for gentle strength training then she'd nap and go back at 4 pm for more swimming. She desperately wanted to be an Olympic swimmer, but unfortunately the pool was only open for five months of the year, and she was shorter than most successful swimmers. She was good, but it was a stretch to think that she could compete at an Olympic level. Throughout primary school, Rowena had continued skiing. She mostly kept up with cross-country, as that is something we enjoyed as a family. When she was 11, a girl on her school's alpine racing ski team broke her arm and they needed another person to complete the team. People knew Rowe had some alpine race experience from Cabramurra Hill and asked her to fill in. She never looked back. From then on all the Bright eyes were turned to the mountains.

A coach from the New South Wales Department of Sport and Recreation in Jindabyne promptly spotted her. He thought she had talent and suggested she be trained. Mum looked into some possibilities and joined the Thredbo Race Club. Some great winters at Thredbo followed. The older kids would be out training for most of the day while mum, Abi and I spent our time at Friday Flat, Thredbo's special beginners area. Kids under the age of five were given free season passes at Thredbo so, in no time, we were riding the Friday Flat chairlift. Mum pulled us up the slope with ropes and then she'd run down behind holding on to the rope around our waists until we could manoeuvre our skis well. As Abi and I progressed, we put on our big red helmets and tucked into a race position skiing straight to the bottom of the slope time and time again. We really felt we ruled the mountains. It wasn't long before we'd graduated from Friday Flat and were exploring all the difficult runs. I remember once, Dad and I were at the top of 'The Bluff', a particularly steep ungroomed run, when a man said to Dad: "You're not going to let that child go down there are you?" I looked up at the man and whispered: "watch me", and took off over that bluff. I was five years old, showing off, carving my way down the mountain effortlessly. The man apparently watched in awe, and dad just smiled and shrugged.

Abi and I were quite the sight at the Thredbo Race Club. We were dishevelled little girls with long ratty blonde hair. Training started early for our older siblings so we'd usually arrive in our PJs having been carried from our beds to our car seats. Mum would feed us in the clubhouse and dress us in our matching, stained, hand-me-down ski suits. They were a yellow khaki colour (reminiscent of diarrhoea by the time they were passed to Abi and I). We were boisterous and often the older kids would egg Abi and I on to see what we would do. We had no fear and always ran circles round them. We also used to kick them in the shins, which I'll admit wasn't very nice, but we all played rough on the mountain and there were lots of laughs. Although she was only knee-high to a grasshopper, Abi behaved as if she owned the mountain. She certainly did not believe in waiting in lift queues. She would wheedle her way through them until she was at the front. Sometimes we would come across her in lesson lines helping the instructors with their children's groups.

It wasn't always smooth sailing on the slopes; we had our fair share of injuries. Ben wanted to spend his eighth birthday on the snow at Thredbo so Rowe and Robin took him for a ride on the 'Crackenback Supertrail'. They were doing a stretch of moguls under the chair and came down from the soft billowy snow onto the rigid cat track meant for traversing across the snow. Rob and Rowe were okay, but poor Ben kneed himself in the chin on landing and bit his tongue in half. There was a two-centimetre hole and blood was pouring all over his face. Robin was a quick thinker and stuffed his mouth with snow and then took him down to mum. She took him to the medical centre only to be told the tongue would heal itself.

Then there was the time Rowe was brought in by her Austrian coach,

Rupert Winkler, who was working at the Thredbo Ski Club. She knocked herself out racing down the mogul field with her group on the last run of the day. Everyone but Rowe had seen a 'DIP' sign at the bottom of the run – she just remembers being elated because everyone had slowed down and that meant she could take the lead. She went full speed into the dip and exploded everywhere. She still has no memory of reaching the bottom of the hill, even though she managed to ski down. She just remembers laying on the clubroom floor with mum and all her brothers and sisters looking over her.

Rowe began training with the NSW Sport and Recreation Team and was awarded scholarships for overseas training. When she was 12 she was the Australian national champion for her age and before she turned 13 she left Australia to compete overseas. She was already top of her age group in Australia and if she wanted to continue she had to take on the US or Europe. She was away from home a lot and she missed us so much. When we would see Rowe off, I used to think that she was going into oblivion; I didn't really understand where Europe was, or what an airport was. I just remember waving at her through the glass, and then she'd disappear.

By the time I was seven, I was doing well with swimming too. I won the freestyle and backstroke southern districts championships that summer. I was a skinny little thing though and I got very cold in the pool when we had early morning training. It was heated but open to the cold Cooma air. I would come out of the water a deep shade of blue. Unlike Rowe, I couldn't keep it up and only trained when the weather was fine. People kept telling mum that I had some natural talent for cross-country skiing. I was also a cross-country running champion so we knew I had the stamina for it. Consequently I began my career in winter sports competing in alpine racing and cross-country skiing. I loved it, but our finances were not abundant. Mum and dad had to be careful. Mum said they tried not to focus on the lack of funds. They said they always expected 'miracles' and received many.

In 1996 Rowena came home from a long trip to Europe with a back injury. She had been training with the Olympic Winter Institute and was completely exhausted. They called it burnout. Years of non-stop training had caught up with her. I guess that's what happens when you have a driven little four-year-old jumping from sport to sport trying to fulfil an Olympic dream. Mum found a natural health nutritionist who took charge of building her system back up. She stopped the distance education program that she had started in Year 8 and took up a half scholarship for year 11 and 12 at the Snowy Mountains Grammar School in Jindabyne. She still worked with NSWIS and her ski team but kept more manageable hours so she could focus on her studies. It was around this time Rowe and I started to become close. I would model for her photography assignments and she would secretly pay me in lollies. Mum still doesn't believe us when we tell her this. We would also workout together at the local gym. Sometimes when we were finished our gym sessions, we'd go out to the car and chow down on chocolate that we'd stashed in the glove box. That's what happens when your health-fanatic mother deprives you of sugar. You have stealth-chocolate-binge-sessions with your older sister. Rowe graduated with extremely good Higher School Certificate (HSC) results, and deferred her acceptance to a degree in media communications at the University of New South Wales. She had recovered well enough to set off again in pursuit of her goal: the Salt Lake City Winter Olympics in three years time. In February of 1998, Rowena had finished thirteenth in the slalom and tenth in the combined at the Junior World Championships in Quebec, Canada. She was on her way again.

I remember going on a road trip from Cooma to Hotham (in Victoria) where Rowena was picking up her gear after a winter of working and training there. Mum let her take me along for company. This car trip was when our beautiful friendship really cemented. We climbed into her little cream 1982 Alpha Romeo Sud, listened to music with our heads out the window, and screamed our favorite songs to the countryside. We laughed our way into each other hearts. We still make each other giddy and laugh about nothing. We think we are the funniest people alive when we are together. I learned so much from Rowe, just by watching the way she lives. She embodies humour, intelligence, generosity and patience. She works with diligence and commitment. She is the most caring, engaged, creative mother. She has shouldered difficulties and disappointments with grace, and a trademark Bright grin. She is an amazing sister, and my best friend.

RUN THREE

'Without leaps of imagination, or dreaming, we lose the excitement of possibilities. Dreaming, after all, is a form of planning.'
– Gloria Steinem

My eldest brother Robin was the first of us to discover snowboarding at Thredbo Race Club. He gave it a whirl with some friends and really enjoyed it. He was also pretty good at it. Mum asked Jason Onley, who was competing in snowboard cross competitions on the world stage, if he would take Robin for a ride. Jason felt Robin had a huge talent. He told mum that with some training and experience Robin could be up there as well. Robin was the first great Bright snowboarder, but sadly, he never went professional.

Many believe that snowboarding is a new sport but in fact primitive boards (resembling a long ski in which you placed both your feet) were being ridden as far back as the 1880s. In the 1960s the first commercial snowboard as we know it arrived. A few guys in Wisconsin in the USA developed a board made of plywood. Tom Sims, a skateboarder, wanted a way to ride during the winter and summer. He made a snowboard at high school (he called it a ski board) and started shredding his way around the snow-adorned city streets. When he began manufacturing and selling his Sims Snowboards, they took off. Jake Burton was likewise creating snowboarding gear that set the standard for the rest of the world. He also introduced snowboarding to the resorts and organized the first National Snowboarding Championships (now known as the US Open) in Snow Valley, Vermont, USA in 1983. Tom Sims won that first World Championship in 1983. These guys, along with others, like Terry Kidwell, battled it out to bring snowboarding to the world. Sims was riding quarter pipes, a lot like skate board ramps. Then he invented the half pipe, which is now one of the most popular snowboard events to watch. In Salt Lake City in 2002, the men's half pipe event was the most watched winter Olympic sport.

Meanwhile, back in Australia, we had our own pioneers. Marcus Wehrle was one of the youngest Australians who took up snowboarding back in 1989. He was active in and around Hotham, the first resort in Australia to allow snowboarding – Hotham also built the first Australian half pipe. Marcus says that in those days, you were just a snowboarder; there was no difference between the pipe guys and the race guys. "The pipe was just two rows of snow piled up," he once told me. "Hermann the cat driver would cut steps along the piles and we would shovel the transitions in. It would take us a few days." The key guys competing back then were Dave Pavlich, Matt Gilder, Steve Toughie, Dave Kelly and Tim Valandis. The two guys to beat were Jason Haynes and 'Burkey'. Doug Atkinson was also a great rider, and Will Mallet's backflip was legendary.

While the half pipe was gaining in popularity, there were members of the snowboarding community who believed that it was the free riding snowboarding (through fresh powder in the wild mountain backcountry) that was the soul of the sport. No matter where I travel, and despite all the different ideas I encounter about what 'snowboarding culture' is, I find that 'shredding' is a universal snowboarding language. It attracts the same fun-loving, free spirited humans everywhere. We just love to shred and explore. It's akin to the culture that can be found in other board sports such as surfing and skateboarding. It comes from a youth street culture, and it bears a different attitude to the elite competitive energy that you find in the ski sports. It's more collegial and more collaborative; it's more of a family. It's a sport that applauds everyone who adventures out and experiments, no matter what results they are getting from judges and competitions.

I remember the first day I tried snowboarding with incredible clarity. It was 1997. I was 11 and the winter season had started really badly. There were very few runs open and those open were covered with mostly man-made snow. Hundreds of people were all crowding the one tiny patch of real snow and it was absolutely boring for us Bright kids. Ben thought trying snowboarding might be interesting in those conditions, so mum hired him a board and organized a lesson. She walked in to the ski school office and asked: "Who is your best snowboarding instructor?" Abi was out on the mountain skiing, but I caught wind of it and got myself included. I will never forget that first lesson. Everything felt so different. When you ski, you wear hard boots that clip into the bindings, but while snowboarding you wear softer boots and ratchet your feet in. On skis, you face straight down the mountain. On a board you face sideways, there's nothing in your hands and no poles to push with. Suddenly I saw the mountain in a completely new light. I followed Ben as he found all the little nooks and crannies to jump off. I went where he went, and took the jumps he took. It was such a rush. Abi was not happy when she returned to find Ben and I in a snowboarding lesson. Because Abi was so upset that she missed out, mum agreed to arrange her a lesson the next day. Ben was off on the mountain but I tagged along for another lesson with Abi. We were completely smitten. After a few two-hour lessons, we were on our way.

RUN THREE

There was a big rivalry between the skiers and the snowboarders in those days. It was akin to the rivalry between surfers and body boarders. We would call snowboarders names, like: 'wanks on planks'. Older skiers felt that snowboarders were dangerous on the slopes and a few resorts around the world banned snowboards from some areas. Even some hire businesses chose not involve themselves in snowboarding. Snowboarders are a different crowd to skiers. I never thought that I would snowboard. Suddenly I was totally thrilled to be a wanker on a plank. When I ski, I want to go fast. I love how much speed I can create to take into turns and through racing gates. When I snowboard, the mountain is like a blank canvas I can paint my way down. Snowboarding ignites my creativity. It is my method of self-expression. Snowboarding for me isn't about getting down the mountain first. It is all about me and my board and what I can push myself to do.

As soon as we came home from our snowboarding lessons, we begged our parents for boards. We went to one of the local stores in Jindabyne and got three set-ups for $150. They were probably about 10 years old but we were thrilled. My board was a Burton Air. It was maroon with a green stripe and a straight tail. Abi's was a little yellow F2 and Ben's was an Elan. The next season Ben, Abi and I were committed snowboarders. We still competed in racing and cross-country skiing for the inter-school events, but we also joined the winter sports club program where we rode with a snowboard team and had a coach. To perfect our trickery, we would unfold a trampoline in the middle of the ski tube building. We would bring the 'trampoline board' out which was an old snowboard with garden hose taped around the sharp edges so the boards wouldn't cut the mat. We would bounce on the boards on the trampolines for hours. We loved it so much we even converted my snowboard at home. Trampolines are great way to cultivate air awareness.

We were so excited and obsessed with snowboarding, that mum gave it a go herself. Ben tried to teach her but she ended up falling over and sustaining a concussion. "No more for me" she said. "I cannot be injured. Mothering is too important!" It was back to the skis for mum. I was pleased I had started out on skis before I tried snowboarding. Learning how to master the four edges of skis definitely gives you the ability to understand a snowboard. That's why I feel we were able to pick it up so easily. We had good edge control skills and it was a simple matter of transferring them to the snowboard. That said though, it's a personal preference whether you chose to put your child on skis or a snowboard when they begin. Skiing worked for me, but I see little shredders only just able to walk being put straight on a snowboard and it's incredible the results they achieve. There is no right or wrong way to do it.

The snow industry in Australia is small, with only two states in which you can participate in snow sports, New South Wales and Victoria. This has resulted in a tight-knit community. There was no shortage of great talent on our slopes. As beginner shredders, Abi, Ben and I made friends with lots of kids like the Allen brothers, Jamie, Clint and Mitch. Mitch went on to compete in the 2006 Winter Olympics half pipe competition. Clint made a great career out of snowboarding and Jamie continued to shred for the love of it while he pursued a trade. Our coach on the winter sports club program, Andrew Burton, also became a 2006 Winter Olympian. When I discovered snowboarding, my life changed. I had a new skill that I was eager to grow, a new group of friends that I loved and a whole new world that I existed in. I lived to shred and explore the mountain.

RUN FOUR

'Every now and then a man's mind is stretched by a new idea or sensation, and never shrinks back to its former dimensions.'
– Oliver Wendell Holmes Sr.

Friendship is the heart of snowboarding culture. The old snow-folk proverb 'no friends on a powder day' doesn't apply to snowboarders. Riding powder is a unique and exhilarating pleasure that you could easily want to keep to yourself. However we believe it's much more exciting if you share it and watch each other enjoy it. Snowboarding is about the experiences you share on the snow. These experiences create amazing bonds and imbue playfulness into your riding style.

When I started snowboarding, I looked up to some excellent female snowboarders: Linda Whitaker, Mandy Woods, Jemima Brain, Katie Brauer and Sasha Rizy. There's nothing better than a great group of women who are united in their passion for something. There were always plenty of female shredders on the mountains. They'd travel from all over New South Wales and Victoria to be there. Some of my favorite days on the mountain were (and still are) with my girlfriends who just love to ride. We rode together, supported each other, and looked out for each other.

Ben has always been obsessed with snowboarding movies. When we

46

were younger, he collected them and watched them fervently. *TB7 North of Heaven*, made in 1997, was his favorite. I wasn't to know then, but watching these films with Ben, provided me with my footing on my own snowboarding ladder to heaven. My mind was opened to a whole new world and I discovered the possibilities of my snowboard. There were so many incredible riders in these videos, but Terje Håkonsen and Tara Dakides were my favorites. You can imagine how I felt when I got an email from Terje a few days after my silver medal in the Sochi 2014 which read: "I saw the final. Haven't seen you ride for a while. It was good to see how much style you've got in your shredding. Too bad judging is so up and down, because I thought you won." Where I'd stood on the podium that day didn't concern me in the least however reading that email was a proud and satisfying moment. It was my style, not my place that made me feel like a winner.

My family would travel across New South Wales and Victoria for the half pipe, big air and snowboard cross events. As we piled into the car, we were always busting to compete. There were the Planet X Games, where international skiers and snowboarders were enticed to come to Australia and compete, with the first prize a week on Sydney's Palm Beach (my favorite of the 'orange sand' northern beaches). There were also the Sprite Sessions, the Coca Cola Classic and the Nintendo Series. We always enjoyed the Nintendo series, as we loved bringing home new consoles and we would do anything we could to earn money to buy games. 'Mario Kart' was my favorite. I loved to be princess peach, Abi was always Bowser and Ben was Toad.

Thredbo's Sprite Sessions snowboard cross was one of my first competitions. I'm so pleased that the bank turns are still there under the Cruiser Chair on the Merritts run. Unlike the freestyle events, all that mattered was who was the first person down. It was about speed and line, and was always a good competitive event. The big air events were my favorites. In big air competitions a jump is constructed with a large take off and landing transition area. The aim is to perform a trick of your choice with as much style and flair of your own; then land it. At the time only a few of the resorts were building half pipes, as they needed a specific machine to cut the transition of the walls.

We became well known on the snowboarding circuit. People started to notice that Ben and I were quite good, even though we had only been in snowboarding events for a few years. I was consistently coming in the top three in my competitions. We had reached the stage where we really needed some better equipment and boards. Over the years we had watched (and learned) as Rowena raised money to supplement her half scholarships with the NSW Department of Sport and Recreation to train to compete overseas. When she was 12 years old she would go from door to door with a pamphlet she had typed up about the evils of tap water. She'd then try to sell people dad's water filters. She would also sell natural bristle toothbrushes and packaged goodies that she and my mum had made, such as healthy trail mixes. She also wrote letters to anyone she could think of. Rowe wrote to Kerry Packer once, not expecting a reply. Mum received a phone call from Colin Rae, the boss of Perisher at that time, stating that he had been instructed by Mr Packer to find out how much Rowena required to get her to Europe. My mum was flabbergasted. Rowe was sent a cheque in the mail and she was on her way. Her first sponsorship deals were with Rossignal, Bolle, Powerbar, and 3M Thinsulate. Later, One.Tel became her major sponsor. I remember being so impressed to see her wear those badges on her ski suits and hats.

Our first paid job was modelling for Manly Blades at the Sydney Ski

Show. It was the middle of summer and all the Bright kids were dressed in one-piece ski suits and Manly Rollerblades. We were on a stage, racing back and forth through gates. We were there to demonstrate to the trade show people how to use rollerblades to train for skiing in the off-season. This was not our most glamorous sponsorship deal. Donning one-piece ski suits in a Sydney summer was about as fun as it sounds. However Bill from Manly Blades was amazing to our family and Rowena still uses the blades he gave her 15 years ago. Just like every good 90s kid, I love blading too.

In 1998 we made some 'Sponsor Me' curriculum vitaes and dropped them into local snowboard shops. We always loved Rhythm Snow Sports shop and would often chat to Mic Klima and Adam Klumper about their gear. Adam was the snowboard shop manager at Rhythm but to us he was the shredding guru. He had spent time in Europe and Alaska snowboarding, and we loved hearing stories about his adventures. Adam took a look at our proposal and asked if he could go for a ride with us. We went up the mountain together that night, and from that moment onwards, Adam was our biggest supporter. We suddenly had all the latest gear. It was heaven. I wore the first jacket that Adam gave me to school because I was so happy and proud. I think other kids thought I was showing off, but I didn't care. My Rhythm jacket became my most prized possession (second only to my snowboard). It wasn't a hand-me-down. It was mine. In return for all the gear they gave us, our job was to hand out 10% discount cards to people on the mountain in lift lines encouraging them to come into Rhythm to rent or buy equipment. We would hand out Minties to help sweeten the deal. We were young and cheeky 'brand ambassadors'.

I have really fond memories of riding with Adam. He would take us out most Tuesday nights. The snow was our stage and we would perform for each other as well as work on the freshly groomed runs. Corduroy is perfect for making beautiful turns. It's called corduroy because of the pattern on the snow that's created after the snow groomer has done a pass on the run. Turning is the first thing you learn and a perfect railed turn on a groomed slope – or a perfect powder turn with billowing snow over your head – is one greatest things in the world. Some nights he got us on race boards and in hard boots. Adam taught us how to hold an edge: "If you can really hold an edge in Australian snow conditions on those things (meaning the race-specific boards we would ride sometimes), you can ride anything," he would say. We picked that up quickly and added the downhill board racing disciplines to our repertoire. The race boards skills helped me later in conquering the half pipe. Mic and Adam gave us everything we needed to be on the mountain doing our thing and I am endlessly grateful. Without their generosity during those early stages, I'm not really sure what would have happened to us. Rhythm Sports still help the local kids in Cooma. The shop is still in the same location and grows every year. They have a Rhythm team and Ben, Abi and I are lifetime members.

Freestyle snowboarding was a whole new world to me. I was learning how to jump, spin, fly and fall. Falling is an important part of learning how to snowboard. Not a day goes by on the mountain where I don't fall and pick myself up, brush myself off and try again. It's a crucial part of the process of mastering a trick. While I mostly avoided injury in those early days (lots of bumps and bruises), one of my falls did leave its mark. I was riding rails with friends. I'd hit the rail and then hike back up and hit it over and over. I fell off the rail early and landed with my hip hitting on the end of the rail. It was slightly dislocated and very painful. I couldn't move while I waited for the train to pull up at the station. I was in excruciating pain. As I limped down the platform to mum, I was whimpering and fighting back tears. The impact had split the fat and muscle layers. To this day my hip still clicks; and I'll forever have a weird lump on my butt.

In 1999 I started high school at Snowy Mountains Grammar School in Jindabyne with a half scholarship. It was a small school with fewer than 100 boys and girls. I wore big glasses and I would sit up the front to see the white board. It was the same thing I had done the in primary school only now I had even bigger glasses. It's the sister school to SCEGS Redlands in Sydney. They had a great winter exchange program. Students from Redlands would come and live on campus in Jindabyne in order to spend time on the mountains during winter and vice versa (snow kids got to experience the city).

In my first year of high school there was an industry trade show at Thredbo. A bunch of snow brands were exhibiting their stuff. Ben introduced himself to Wes Fab from Burton and Nick Wright from Arnette. He informed them that he and I were good snowboarders and that they should sponsor us. He recalls they laughed and said they needed to see some results first. That season we competed in all the events throughout New South Wales and Victoria. At the Nintendo Event at Hotham in Victoria, Nick Wright got to see those results he was asking for. The Bright kids cleaned up. We brought home a Nintendo and a few hundred dollars cash. After seeing us ride, Nick took a pair of orange 'Swingers' out of his bag and gave them to me. They were so big on my little pin-head. I looked ridiculous but I didn't care; I was sponsored. A little later Burton came on board for me too, in conjunction with Rhythm Sport.

During the southern winter of 1999, we were suddenly being offered a variety of sponsorship deals. Jason Haines, a rider from Quiksilver at the time, invited me to Sydney to meet Mark Rayner who was the Quiksilver/ Roxy Team Manager. I was so excited I couldn't contain myself. I decided to get a new haircut for the occasion and tried to calm my nerves. Roxy was a brand I really believed in (and still do). I loved their gear and I respected the way they supported their athletes. I really wanted them to like me. The meeting went well and before I knew it, I was sponsored by Roxy. We were still a part of the winter sports club program and were receiving mentoring from notable people in the snowboard world. So we were being supported on both sides of the industry.

Sponsorship was a dream come true, however my greatest sponsors have always been my parents. Dad and mum sacrificed a lot to keep us all on the mountain. Lift tickets, travel to different resorts for competitions, accommodation, and entry fees were all very expensive. My father worked incredibly hard. He worked from sun up to sun down and had to travel long distances for work. He often wouldn't be home in time for dinner. He also worked for himself. This meant he had to manage all the trials and tribulations incumbent on a small business owner. Mum had to take on a second job one winter to help keep us all going. We stayed with friends in Jindabyne until we moved into a small apartment while she worked every day. It was the only way she could look after her children and keep us on the mountain. I don't think mum and dad would change anything now. They did what they thought they needed to do to this to give us the opportunity to 'magnify our talents'. The saying 'behind one great athlete there is an even greater team', rings particularly true for me. My family have always grounded me. You could say they are my 'strength of ten'.

RUN FIVE

'Don't let anyone rob you of your imagination, your creativity, or your curiosity. It's your place in the world; it's your life. Go on and do all you can with it, and make it the life you want to live.'
– Dr. Mae Carol Jemison

I was 13 years old and the 2000 Sydney Summer Olympics were just around the corner. Unbeknownst to me, my school friends had submitted a nomination for me to carry the torch as a representative of our local area. I was surprised and elated when I opened the letter inviting me to bear the torch. It was such an incredible honour. I ran the torch through a town outside of Cooma called Bredbo. At the time Rowena was preparing for the Winter Olympics in 2002 and Olympic aspirations had also started to germinate in me.

Our dreams aside, we loved the Olympics and everything it stood for. It is an event that unites and celebrates humanity. Six colours symbolize all countries, and remind us of our universality. What is important is not to win, but to come together, to prepare and to participate. Athletes compete with dignity on a world stage, and nations unite to encourage and enjoy their athlete's effort. Once it was a tribute to the twelve gods of Olympus, today it captures the hearts of millions of people on earth. I love the history, the mythology and the way it brings people together.

Our family drove together to Sydney that September to soak up the atmosphere of the host city. The city was electric. Thousands crowded together to watch events on big screens erected around the city. The sound of cheering vibrated through the streets. I could feel the heartbeat of the city. It was alive in a way I'd never seen it before. It was intoxicating.

On the 26th December the same year, Ben and I left for our first trip together overseas. Things had started to change very fast. By now we had lots of support from our sponsors – Rhythm in Cooma, Burton, Arnette, Roxy, and Quiksilver. Arnette funded an airfare for Ben and I and Roxy allowed me a small travel budget. However we were not completely financially independent. We had to find the funds for accommodation and incidentals. We had no fixed plans. It was very exciting. We only knew one detail for certain. We had to be in Italy in March of 2001. We had both qualified to be in the Junior World Championships in snowboarding in Sappada.

Before we left we shared an Australian Christmas Day lunch at the beach in Sydney with our (might as well be) family, the Sharps. We often spent summers with the Sharps. Jan Sharp is mum's best friend. She has three children around the same ages as the eldest Brights – Natasha, Niki and Ben. We spent a few Christmases there, everyone sleeping in the living room together, waking up together on Christmas morning and exchanging gifts. Jan Sharp is an incredible woman; how she put up with hosting all of us I don't know. Jan always helped out whenever any of us needed to be in Sydney. Ben and I had never left the country before and it was our first time on a plane. I was equal parts nervous and thrilled. Mum, dad and Abi came to the airport and saw us off. Now there were three Brights, playing in the international competitive snowfields of the world. It felt so surreal. I had stood up against the glass window of the airport and waved my big sister off year after year, now I was actually in her world; now I knew she did not just disappear.

Our friend, Jenny O'Donnell, had invited Ben and I to join her in Big White in Canada. They had previously let Rowena use their apartment in Hotham for a season. Her children, Pip, Jess and Cara, trained in their various disciplines too. We all became good friends. I hadn't heard of Big White, and had no idea where it was. We landed in Kelowna in British Columbia and made our way there with the O'Donnells. The next day was my 14th birthday and mum told me not to tell them, otherwise they would feel obliged to do something for me. She felt that they were already doing enough by giving us a place to stay. The next day we woke up and went straight to the mountain to get our lift tickets sorted. I was required to write my birthday on the application form for the season pass. I dutifully filled in the form trying to be discreet but Jess saw it and said "Torah, it's your birthday today, Why didn't you tell us?" That night they made a cake for me. It was so lovely of them, but the opportunity they offered us really was the best present I could have hoped for. I rode the mountain on my birthday. It was breathtaking. I was in complete awe of this new place and all the snow I had at my fingertips to shred and explore.

Eventually the O'Donnells went home and we needed to find new accommodation. Ben was having a great time on the mountain in Big White so he stayed on there for a while couch-snowboarding (like couch-surfing but better). An Australian all girls' action sports magazine called Chick Magazine wanted to take me to Whistler, Canada for an editorial shoot. Mark Rayner, my Roxy Team Manager, organized payment for my airfares and transport to get me there. Katie Brauer would be travelling with me. I flew to Vancouver to meet Katie and we caught a bus up to Whistler. Linda Whitaker, Jess Mooney, and Richard Hegarty were also on the shoot with us. Katie Brauer had some friends, Bec and Bo Graig, in Whistler and asked them if they would mind if I crashed temporarily on their couch. They welcomed me without batting an eyelid. I was very grateful. I can't remember how long I stayed but they, and their lizard I shared the living room with, were very gracious. I run into Bo at industry trade shows from time to time and it's always great to see him.

Whistler is known for its amazing parks and completely stunning sprawling backcountry. We explored the backcountry on snowshoes, hiking and walking to find the natural features on the mountain to jump off. I was riding features I had never ridden before. We worked hard on the mountain every day to get enough locations and angles for the magazine. It was such a rush to ride with women I admired. When we'd wrap for the day, I loved going out to dinner and relaxing with the gang. One night I was dared to eat a chunk of wasabi the size of a golf ball. I find it hard to resist a dare. My stomach felt like it was burning for two days afterwards. Wasabi bravado aside, I was having an amazing time and I didn't want to leave. I discovered that another Australian snowboarder, Belinda Olding from Sydney, was at Whistler too. My sister knew Belinda from the Snowy Mountains Grammar School. She was a racer; giant slalom on the snowboard. She had a studio apartment in Whistler that she let me share with her. It particularly generous as she only had one room. I also joined in on the race training that she was doing. Looking back, I can't believe how lucky I was. There were so many people who put themselves out to help a teenager stay on the mountain and snowboard. The kindness of friends played a principal role in me moving on to the world stage.

I took the opportunity to compete in lots of local events and was delighted to be awarded podium positions in the international arena. I didn't feel like I needed to prove myself. I just enjoyed myself and did what came naturally to me, just as I had done back home in the mountains of Australia. Before long I began to be noticed by international riders. "Who's that young girl hitting big jumps?" people started to ask. I could pretty much hit any size jump but I hadn't learned any major tricks. I could hit the rails and do grabs but I hadn't started spinning really. It was incredible to learn how to rotate. I would hike a little jump over and over again doing 360s and adding different types of grabs. Anthony Krute and his wife Karen used to ride with me at Whistler. Sadly, Anthony has since passed. He was such a wonderfully spirited man. He taught me how to do my first backside 360. That backside 360 helped me place runner up in the Sims World Championship in Vail USA.

Eventually Ben and I reunited and set off together for Europe. It was our first trip to the continent. We were headed to St Moritz. We wanted to spend some time in Switzerland training together before we ventured to Sappada where we were due to compete. Unfortunately, one of our flights was delayed and we had to sleep in the fluorescent-lit comfort of an airport burger joint. We reached Zurich much later than planned and were supposed to take a train from Zurich to St. Moritz. We set off on our journey and prepared to change trains as we were told, in a town called Chur, but because we had been delayed, we missed the last train. We were stuck, it was late, we were in a foreign country, and we couldn't speak Swiss German or German. We ventured out of the train station to find a hotel when suddenly a pack of kids ran up to us in black masks. They shouted at us and poked at our bags. I was terrified, I thought we were getting mugged. Finally we found an elderly couple that we managed to communicate to that we needed a place to stay. They put us in a taxi to a hotel. It had a bar downstairs so Ben made me get out of the taxi and wait outside with our luggage while he went to see if they had a room.

RUN FIVE

I was exhausted, my nerves were shaken and I was feeling a little homesick. Then out of the hotel waltzed Andrew Burton with a bunch of our friends from the snowboard circuit in Australia. I screamed and threw my arms around them. It was such a welcome surprise. They had come into Chur after snowboarding all day to experience the Swiss Carnival of Fasnacht. We realized then that the kids we'd encountered earlier were probably just part of the parade. I was eager to hear all about Andrew's evening. Ben eventually returned to take me to the room he'd booked for us so we said our goodbyes. I've never been so excited to see a bed.

When we finally made it to St Moritz, we were fortunate to stay with more friends, the Baffs. Peter, Trina and their first daughter, Georgia, lived and worked in St Moritz during the winters. We were in the Swiss Alps, the Engadeen valley, home to Michi Albin – the Pontrrecenia destroyer. He was another of our shredding heroes. We spent our time riding and exploring the mountain and, lucky for us, we happened to be in Switzerland during one of the best snowfalls in 50 years. I had never seen anything like it. The streets were covered with snowdrifts and there were snow banks as tall as buses. The terrain was so accessible from the lifts, I was able to get straight off the lift and ride little lines right under the gondola.

Gregory Oteeves, a snowboard student of Peter Baff's, accompanied Ben and I on our explorations and adventures. Gregory organized for a helicopter to pick us up and take us to the top of the mountain. It was incredible to experience a bird's eye view of the valley. Meanwhile, Rowena had just finished up in the World Ski Racing Championships in St Anton in Austria. She had finished 14th in the combined event before coming down with a terrible flu for the rest of her events. Despite that, her one result allowed her to qualify for the Winter Olympics in Salt Lake City in 2002. I was so pleased to hear she had achieved one of her dreams.

RUN FIVE

She was on the Olympic team. After the world championships, she had a race in Lenzer Heidi, Switzerland, which was only an hour's drive away from St Moritz so Rowe came and stayed for a night with us. The next day I drove back with her and saw one of her races.

Rowe turned up again a few weeks later with a car her sponsor One.Tel had given her and drove Ben and I from St Moritz to Sappada, Italy. It took us about three hours. She dropped us off for training and then stayed with us, sleeping in my bed so she could watch Ben and I compete in our events. It was such an amazing treat that she was able to be with me. Before the ISF Junior World Championships started, the Italians were holding their own FIS National Championships. I was entered in the snowboard cross event and I placed second in the open women's category. It was a huge morale boost for me going into the ISF Juniors. I had placed second in my first major international competition. Everyone competing at the Junior Worlds was under 18 years of age. We came from all corners of the globe, united by our love of snowboarding. I was competing in the half pipe and boarder cross. There was a huge group of young Australian snowboarders in Italy ready to compete in what turned out to be the last year of the ISF Junior World Championship. The Junior Worlds in Sappada that year was star studded with global industry leaders – Danny Kass, Heikki Sorsa, and riders who would later be my teammates; Kjersti Buaas, Margot Rozie, Mathieu Crépel. It felt wonderful. I was in awe of all these snowboarders and now I was competing alongside them. Sappada was also home to Italian snowboarding brothers, Filippo and Giacomo Kratter, aka 'the Italian stallions'. They were such characters in the snowboard world and gnarly shredders too. They were absolutely wild and went out of their way to show all the young party-goers at this junior worlds how to have a good time.

RUN FIVE

During the competition, Ben suffered an injury in the hotel rather than the pipe. He'd been out all night but before he hit the hay, he decided it would be a really good idea to play knock-and-run on every room on every floor of the hotel. To reach each new floor he jumped whole flights of stairs at a time. Speed was of the essence in this game. He had managed to turn knock-and-run into an extreme sport. On his way down to the first floor, he jumped a little too high and hit the front of his head on the low roof of the stairs above. As he hit the ground he smashed the back of his head on the bottom stair. Rowe and I came out to find him swearing and growling in pain on the floor surrounded by a pool of blood. He had split the front and back of his head. The lighter side of the debacle was that Ben, who had these massive blonde medusa-like curls at the time, had to shave a patch so he could get stitches. It looked hilarious. Everyone thought it was a wonderful idea for him to shave a little more off and leave three tufts so that he looked like 'Krusty the Clown'. He did so, but to my disappointment, he didn't dye the tufts turquoise.

Benny ended up in eighth place in the half pipe. He had the tricks and skills to place a lot better and I remember Rowe and I being so disappointed for him when we watched him crash some of his tricks. However it was still an impressive result. Eighth in the world is extremely respectable. Mathieu Crépel came seventh and Gary Sebrowski won the event. I was competing in the lower category in the under 14s. Competing doesn't faze me. I am good at it. I have been competing since I was three years old. I have always known how to balance the expectations and the pressures from my self (and those around me) while also harnessing the joy. We were required to do two runs, with the best run taken as your score for the event. We had a few training days for the event. On those days I was feeling the pipe out, riding the only way I knew how: fearless and free.

RUN FIVE

On the day of the competition, it was overcast, foggy and moist. Rowe sat at the bottom of the pipe watching me. I don't remember much about the run but it must have been okay because I placed third. Realizing I was third in the world gave me an incredible high. I really wanted to talk to mum and dad, and I didn't have to wait long. A journalist, Burgit Gruber, at the bottom of the pipe had a mobile phone and asked me if I wanted to call my parents. Rowe dialled the number and put me on the phone. It was in the middle of the night in Australia but my parents were thrilled to hear from me and hear of the great result. It was my first international benchmark. I adamantly maintain that no contest result defines your ability as a snowboarder, but this result did validate that I had talent and that it was perhaps worth seeing where I could take snowboarding. I also felt that it was my gift to the people who had helped and supported me. I wanted them to be proud of me.

After the last ever ISF Junior World Championships, Ben and I had a few days in Venice with Fergus Munroe and his father, Mike. People dream of visiting Venice, and here Ben and I were able to have another amazing life experience before heading home to Australia. It was a huge cultural awakening. We rode gondolas, ate fabulous Italian pizza, enjoyed gelato on the canals, visited the Peggy Guggenheim Museum, and were exposed to some of the richest art history. Life was grand for two Cooma-kids.

When we arrived home it was back to school for us. I was in year 8 and Ben was in year 10. I was exhausted by the trip. I fell asleep during one class and woke up with my face in the middle of a puddle of drool. I was so embarrassed, but I couldn't control my fatigue. It was hard to catch up on all the schoolwork that I had missed. Other schooling options needed to be looked at. More importantly, where was I going for the next northern winter? It was clear that I needed to move out of Australia and immerse myself in the industry. It's hard in Australian winter sports. If you want to take it seriously, you have to spend time in the northern winter too. Australian facilities just weren't good enough (nor was the winter long enough) for us to be able to train and learn and compete at an international level. Things are very different now as the Australian resorts are putting a lot of resources in the winter action sports realm. However the hub of industry for action sports is still in North America and Europe and that's where you need to be. I had suffered from homesickness while I was away and would have loved to have remained at home and finished school surrounded by my friends and family. However I sacrificed my want for what I (rightly) suspected was my future. I began to plan my half-yearly expat life.

2000–2001 Season

2nd Place – FIS National Championships, Italy, Boardercross – 2001

3rd Place – ISF Junior World Championships, Superpipe – 2001

RUN SIX

'You may be disappointed if you fail, but you are doomed if you don't try.'
– Beverly Sills

In November 2001 I packed my bags again. My coach at the time, Ben Wordsworth, spent his northern winters at Mammoth Mountain, a snow resort in California. He suggested I could live at Mammoth for the winter and ride with the mammoth snowboard team. Ben found a family, the Behlers, who were willing to give me a home for the winter. This time, along with my snow equipment, I packed six months worth of textbooks. I was about to miss the first half of the school year. We travelled to Sydney airport. After bear hugs all around, I took off for Los Angeles.

I had engaged my first agent before I left, Paul Malina. Paul had reached an elite level in freestyle rollerblading. He got me a spot on a TV show I loved at the time, *The Panel* (a show where bunch of comedians and celebrities sat around and talked about stuff). Paul and I met in person for the first time in Melbourne before the show went live. His brother, Dave Malina, was heading the LA branch of IMS Sport. Dave met me in LA and drove me the six hours from LA to Mammoth Mountain where I met up with my (wonderful) new host family. It is a breathtaking drive to Mammoth. There are miles and miles of fault lines where the land just drops away. It's a wild countryside and the snow on the mountains is clean and crisp. Mammoth Mountain is 11,053 feet above sea level, about 3000 feet higher than Mount Kosciusko, Australia's highest. It is an active volcano area, and you can feel little grumbles underneath. Nobody seemed to worry much about that, (I found it pretty strange though). I guess the magnificence of the Sierra Nevadas drowns out the fear of any submerged instability. As soon as I met Kayla and her mum Bev, I just knew I would be fine, they were great. Kayla was also on the Mammoth snowboard team. She introduced me to people and showed me around town. I loved my snowboard team at Mammoth and we all became fast friends. Little did I know I was snowboarding with people who would go on to be some of the greatest snowboarders of our time: Eric Jackson, Mason Aguirre, Danny Kass and Eric's brother, John Jackson.

Distance education meant I had to schedule all my study myself. I had to study hard at night after my days on the mountain to keep up with the assignments. I tried my best but it became difficult when I was invited on trips and to events. I was travelling a lot. The exercise books weighed heavily on my mind (and desk). Six weeks flew by and I celebrated my first Christmas away from home. Not having my family with me was much more difficult that I had expected. My dad's birthday is the 26th of December and mine is the 27th so mum always made it a three-day celebration. It was also my first white Christmas but instead of 'dreaming' I was drowning in homesickness. It was all backwards. Christmas is meant to be boiling hot, and you're meant to eat salad and seafood and cool off in the ocean or under sprinklers. This 'hot dinner' and 'rugging up' business felt strange to me, (no matter how ridiculously beautiful it looks or how many songs have been written about it). My big brother came to my rescue. He was travelling to the US and on to Canada and could spend some time

Early competition days

Finding my first legs with Rowena   Hungry after a day on the farm

Mum with Robin (left) and Rowena (right)

The Bright Family: Robin, Dad, Torah, Benny, Mum, newborn Abi and Rowena

On my cross-country skis at Thredbo Ski Club

On two planks where the mountain adventures all began

Digging trenches on my race board

Cross-country
running day

Farm days, wishing I
could ride the motor
bike

Ben and I – friends from the start

Ben and I –
always buds
on the snow

Adoring my baby sister, Abi

With family, Left to right: Ben, Robin, Abi and Rowena, 1999

With grandparents Ronnie and John Davidson and Abi

Happy to be receiving an award
from Winter Olympic bronze
medalist Zali Stegal

X Games win, Aspen, 2009

Getting comfy in our 2006 Olympic uniforms

With Benny at the X Games, 2007

First hit in the Olympic pipe, backside 360, Torino, Italy, 2006

Most useful trophy I have ever won: best combined performance, US Open, 2008

Infinite love and gratitude from my mother Marion at North Head,
Sydney

Summer fun on the Lake with Neena Earl, Alicia Wade and Jann Neilson.

Bright girls! Back left to right: Rowena, Marion,; Front left to right: Abi,
Torah

With Richard Hegerty (left), Holly Crawford and Mathieu Crepel at the
Junior Worlds, Italy, 2001

Smile. Morocco with my new friend, 2008

Port Douglas sun
and ocean with
Mumma Bright

TWINS! Nicaragua
with Rowena

Obi cuddles with nephew, Lyon

Checking in the brave
Syd as an unaccompanied
minor to fly home after
a Californian adventure,
April 2004

Olympic test event with Scotty Lago at
Sochi, Febuary, 2013

in Mammoth Mountain with me after Christmas. I was delighted to see him.

The New Year arrived which meant we were finally in 2002, Rowe's Winter Olympics year. I celebrated New Yeas Eve at a friend's party. As the clock turned to 12, I had a little pash with Steven Myers. Sadly, instead of embracing the opportunity (he was pretty cute) and enjoying a winter-fling, I got really shy and spent the rest of the season trying very hard to channel *When Harry Met Sally* (minus the getting-together-at-the-end bit). In early February, mum, dad and Abi arrived in Mammoth. The next day we hit the road. We travelled across the Nevada desert headed to Salt Lake City and Rowe. We arrived just in time to enjoy the opening ceremony on TV with the family of Kurt and Mary Kay Fortie, friends of Rowe's from Austria who were providing us with their basement apartment to stay in. Salt Lake City swelled with the spirit of community. So many of the families were offering accommodation, meals and cars to athletes and families without any interest in remuneration.

We had a sensational time and were busy from early in the morning until late at night. Salt Lake City knew how to throw a party. Everything was buzzing. Because we were an athlete's family, we had special entry to many areas. I tried to get tickets to see the half pipe event held at Park City Resort, about 35 minutes out of Salt Lake City but I missed out. It was the most popular event at the games, both live and on TV. I was glad people were finding it so exciting. The gold medal that Kelly Clark won that year in the half pipe was the first of her three Olympic medals. The pipe was superb and the performances matched the facility. I would come to do much training (and competing) in that very pipe in succeeding years.

Mum was astounded by how delightfully pleasant the police and other authority figures were. A traffic jam caused by a broken down bus held us up while we in transit to Rowe's first event. We looked out the window and Mitt Romney (who was brought in to head the Games after some managerial difficulty some months earlier) was out on the road directing traffic. We travelled north of Salt Lake City along the Wasatch Mountain range for 90 minutes to Snowbasin Mountain Resort for Rowe's event. It was really foggy at the top in the morning so the downhill racing leg was postponed until the afternoon. Instead, the slalom leg, starting half way down the hill, was run first.

The atmosphere of anticipation is already immense at the Olympics, and it's magnified when you know your loved one is on the course. We were all having multiple litters of kittens. Rowe came out of the start gate, charging aggressively, taking the tightest line she could. Some of us were shouting her on while the rest of us sat in anxious silence. In the last section of the race, she came over a knoll into the steep pitch just a little too tightly and straddled a gate between her legs. Both legs have to go around the gate so this meant she was disqualified. Our hearts all fell. Her Olympic debut was done. A millisecond later we saw her head bow and then look left up the hill at the gates she had just flown past. Rowena hiked back up the hill, completed the missed gates correctly and finished the race. She came in dead last and would stay in that position for the downhill leg. She was not really in the race anymore. There was no way to make up the time, but she did it to finish.

Her dejection was intense, but looking back, she tells me she is so happy she made that split second decision to pick herself up and finish the race, to fight to the end. As a mother, she uses that story to encourage her children to never give up, to do their best no matter what the outcome and to finish whatever they start. Which is really what the Olympics is all about. The story pertinently illustrates that sometimes we'll suffer disappointments, and that's okay too. We pick ourselves up and just keep going.

RUN SIX

I had never seen her do the fast downhill with jumps before. Rowena used to say that of all the sports she did, ski racing was the most challenging and amazing. She said you needed the speed and power of a sprinter, the agility and flexibility of a gymnast, the precision of a rally car racer, the focus of a golfer, and a whole lot of fearlessness. As I watched, I agreed. It was pretty awe-inspiring. I remember watching her and being so stoked at the big air she got off some of the downhill jumps. I said, "Rowe you got the biggest air out of everyone… you were amazing." She replied "Yeah that's actually a bad thing in downhill to get the most air… but thanks. I love you, Torah Jane." We all laugh now and think it's pretty special to have someone in the family who came last in the Olympics and someone who came first.

Rowe's next event, the slalom, combined the times of two runs down a tightly gated course. It is a very technical event requiring fast edge changes and the use of your strength and power to make the gates. This time we travelled west in the range to Deer Valley (one of the resorts that never allowed snowboarding). It had been a warm night and the course had not frozen properly so after a few runners, the course began to get huge holes in it. By the time Rowe's turn came, there were holes and new snow on the course, which renders it slower, and more challenging. If you didn't go down in the top ten, you really didn't have a chance. The coach had told her to go a bit easy to make sure of a second run, as skiers were coming out all over the place. She gauged it wrongly in the snowy conditions and was too slow. As soon as she finished, she knew she should have just gone for it, quite a different circumstance to her first event. Rowe and I know that our alpine workplaces (with wind and snow and ice and ever-changing conditions) are dangerous. Athletes do sustain serious injuries and some lose their lives. You have to meet the conditions with intelligent planning and the courage to put your plan into action or to pull out. She played it safe that day but you have to be prepared to make such choices in this industry.

Disappointments aside, we all had a magical Olympic experience. We partied hard with other Aussie competitors' families that were there and some friends from Australia who had flown over too. The highlight of those Olympics was when Australian Steven Bradbury won gold in the short track speed skating. As a child, Rowena had hoped she would win Australia its first Winter Olympic gold medal. While things didn't turn out quite that way, she was beyond ecstatic that she was there to watch Bradbury make history. We all were, everyone was bursting with pride and there was much celebration. Sadly I had to leave Salt Lake City early as Roxy wanted me to attend an event in Colorado. We had loved being together to celebrate all Rowe's years of hard work, courage and determination. Mum, dad and Abi dropped me back at Mammoth and flew on home.

Shortly after the Winter Olympics, my representation had a slight reshuffle. Dave Malina, who was looking after me in the US, hired Circe Wallace. We instantly hit it off. She took over all my negotiations. Circe was a pioneer. She was one of the first women who really made snowboarding a career. I had always admired her work in films I'd seen. She was one of the first female snowboarders who rode alongside the male snowboarders. She was a backcountry girl and was one of the only women on Air Walk. She had friends like Barrett Christy and Tara Dakides. Circe Wallace was not only a great sports agent, she was a legend and she was going to represent me.

I had started to feel increased performance pressure. I had to fulfil my obligations to both Burton Snowboards and Roxy at photo shoots and any other appearances. I was earning real money from sponsorship that Circe was negotiating for me, which meant I had to lift my game constantly. I had to get my head around the world competition circuit for snowboarding as well. As I was sponsored by private companies, I was really in the professional world. If you are on the professional tour, you go on the TTR and X Games and Dew Tour events. Then if you want to compete in the Olympics, you need to compete in FIS Tour events, to earn points towards Olympic qualifications. Some people just go on the FIS Tour to qualify for the Olympics the year prior to the games. This is what I chose to do to manage my professional career and obligations. This separation between the two competition circuits is still something I don't agree with. It's something that Terje Håkonsen, and the shredding forefathers, also struggled with early on in their careers. The divide segregates our countries' talent and stunts progression of the athletes. We are currently trying to create our own riders' union that will ultimately govern our sport.

In June to July 2002, I went to Oregon's Mount Hood for a summer camp to do some summer riding for both Roxy and Burton. It was there that I had my first major injury which took five months to recover from. I had packed up for the day (including my gloves) and was just riding back to the car. The girls in front of me were calling out "rocks!" but it was too late; I'd already hit one. I shot forward from my board about five meters from the car park and landed in the snow on my bum. My friend Shaun White came up behind me to see if I was okay and I looked up at him laughing. His face just dropped and he pointed at my hand. It was covered in blood with a loose flap of skin pulsing blood. He took his shirt off and wrapped up my hand.

The medical team checked me out and took me to the local hospital. I had severed a tendon in my right hand, which required some hand surgery in Portland Oregon. My Burton Team Manager, Sean Lake, drove me there.

I flew back to California and stayed with Circe for a while and then flew home to Australia to start hand rehab. My hand needed to be in a splint for about three months as the tendon repair was very delicate. It was my Australian winter and I wasn't allowed to ride. I couldn't even have a shower without the splint on. Thank goodness for liquid soap. The upside was that I could catch up on schoolwork. I learned how to write with my left hand and used a computer with my left hand as well. I'm now quasi-ambidextrous which I'm pretty pleased about. I learned that winter, that being injured isn't just about resting; it's a whole journey of discovery. I really enjoyed hitting the books again and I worried that the northern winter had all been a bit too much. I wondered whether I should take snowboarding more casually for a few years, finish school and then see how I felt. Then, right on cue, the phone rang. Mum called out to me, "It's Circe, and she is asking if you are sitting down." I sat down. Burton had offered me a head-to-toe contract that stipulated that by the fourth year I would be earning a six-figure income. This threw a spanner in the works. I had to make some big decisions about my future. Firstly, was I going to continue snowboarding professionally? Secondly, was I leaving Roxy?

Roxy immediately matched the offer. I decided quickly that I did want to stay in the game and so was left only with the harrowing decision of which sponsorship contract to take up. The choice between Roxy and Burton was incredibly difficult. Both companies had meant a lot to me over the years. The thought of making a decision made me feel sick. I put it off as long as I could. I took lots of walks and did a fair share of soul-searching. Circe, Roxy and Burton became more than a little frustrated wanting for my answer.

Anyone who has followed my career knows how this particular story ends. I'm a Roxy woman through and through. I decided to stay with Roxy because they are like a family to me. They are my riding partners, my team managers and my friends. Roxy was the original women's board sports brand and prides itself on being true to its core, the mountains and the ocean. I also liked how Roxy treated their riders when they changed their career trajectory. The athletes are (and always have been) the soul of the company. Retired athletes are still brand ambassadors to this day.

Rowena was making big decisions too. She was offered an athletic scholarship to study at the University of Utah and compete with their ski team in Salt Lake City. Accepting the scholarship would mean that she would have to finish with the Australian ski team. It was a big step and one that she did not take lightly. She definitely had not reached her potential in ski racing but, with some loss of sponsorship and mediocre results at the Olympics, she felt that it was time to move on. It was a decision that would change the course of her life. She enrolled in an interior design degree with a minor in English. Returning to study suited her, she rediscovered her love of art and felt energized at living a life-of-the-mind again. In many ways she got the best of both worlds. She was in an environment where she could nourish her intellect and her passion for skiing. I was a little envious; I was missing school and hoped to go to university one day too (I still do). However I knew that I'd likewise made the right choice. I had to make the most of my gifts, and give it my best shot, whatever the outcome, just as Rowe had done.

It became clear that I needed someone to travel with me, help me with my schoolwork, and drive me to competitions. My amazing mother and father knew that I needed more than a personal assistant and decided that while I was still a teenager, what I really need was my mother by my side. I needed strategic help, but I also needed emotional support. This has remained true throughout my career, and why in the future Benny would become my 'super coach'.

Mum packed up her life in Cooma and she and Abi came with me. I was so incredibly happy that I would have at least part of my family near me. Where to go was the easy part. Rowe was committed to spending at least 4 undergraduate years in Utah so it was a no-brainer that we'd find somewhere to live near her. With an international airport fifteen minutes out of the city, five world-class snow resorts and a competitive snow industry, it was just right for Abi and I. We also had lots of friends in the snowboard world living in Salt Lake City. The world-renowned resort at Park City has great freestyle facilities, which really suited me. In the summer there are national parks all over Utah. The majesty of Lake Powell deserves reverence, Zions and Arches national parks are utterly gorgeous, Moab is great for mountain biking, the San Raphael Swell perfect for rock climbing. I also adore the American Fork Canyon, and Crystal Hot Springs. It honestly has everything I love except the ocean. It was the perfect move. Mum, Abi and I set up a home in a little basement apartment that Rowe had found for us in Salt Lake City. Our house was only a 20-minute drive from the mountains, which meant that we could be on the mountain all day.

Every day mum drove us to the mountain and would then spend her day in the car organizing correspondence school work and other admin while Abi and I rode. Mum also drove us to competitions and magazine shoots. Abi's professional career was starting to take off and she had obligations to her own sponsors which mum also helped her meet. She was a Billabong shredder on Endeavor boards. Ben was in Europe with his sponsors, busy with competitions and magazine shoots. Dad and Robin were left at home. Dad missed us, but loved his work in the great outdoors and, by that time, Robin was married with a beautiful baby girl, Janaya.

There wasn't a world tour for snowboarders at that time. Now we have the TTR World Tour (Ticket To Ride), but back then, we'd just compete in lots of individual events, like the X Games, the Global Open Series and the Van's Cup. I spent the 2002–2003 northern winter season going from event to event. We travelled a lot between California, Utah and Colorado and flew to New England, Canada, Japan and Europe for other big competitions and photo shoots for my different sponsors. Sometimes it was for their catalogues, in which they liked to have their athletes modelling their gear, and other times it was for action shoots.

Photo shoots aren't too dissimilar from training sessions; we watch each other and experiment. I was also studying films and trying out the tricks I saw, which meant a lot of falling over, picking myself up and trying again. I watched riders and friends like Hampus Mosesson, from Sweden, and Danny Kass, a US rider, in the half pipe. I find that if I can see the trick in my head before I try it out, I can do it with my body. It's sort of a phenomenological training meditation. There are heaps of different ways to learn. I am a visual learner and a kinesthetic feeler. At one photo shoot in June Mountain, California, at the end of 2002, I was riding with kids my own age. Scotty Lago, a future bronze medallist at the Vancouver Olympics, was there with his dad. His father taught me a new trick, a McTwist, in the half pipe. To this day, it's my favorite. I also learned to do a cab 540 on a jump with my friend and teammate, Amber Stackhouse. A great deal of tricks and skills are exchanged and shared in the snowboarding family.

I was competing in all sorts of events and I was doing well, riding hard and loving life. In the US Open of snowboarding, I placed sixth in slopestyle. Slopestyle is an obstacle course made up of different jumps and rail features. You make your way down with trickery and style. Sometimes there are as many as four jumps and four rail features in a course. The courses are always different depending on the events. That's what makes it one of the most exciting events to compete in. It's always dynamic and challenging.

Mum knew we would need to have a good vehicle to get around in and negotiated the Roxy contract to include for us to have a car. My first car was a Silver Toyota Forerunner, but there was one problem, I didn't have my license. Luckily you can hold a license at 16 in Utah, so I sat the test as soon as I could and was behind the wheel. It's funny to me that as an Aussie kid, I ended up learning to drive on the right-hand side of the road. Mum and Abi had to leave in March 2002. Abi was not yet set up to study through distance education and they did not have visas to remain in the US any longer. I was sad to see them go. They had been such a great support.

I was 16 years old and suddenly had no parental supervision and a brand new set of wheels. I drove Mum and Abi to the airport in my own car. I had obtained my license the day before they left so it was my first solo drive coming back from the airport. It was a great feeling. I put on some music, turned it up, and wound down the windows. I was finally independent. Having wheels meant I could now drive myself to the mountain, to visit my friends and I could take myself on adventures. A whole world of possibilities was opening up before me.

Ever since I was 11 years old, I dreamed of being totally independent. I wanted to have something of my own. I loved flowers and I have a strong creative streak. I thought I would run a flower shop. Dad's father's family had been florists; his grandmother had started in the great depression with a business in North Sydney that remained in the family for three generations. They had flower-farming land at St Ives in Sydney. My budding snowboarding career turned out to be my blossom instead, and my creativity wasn't neglected, it was being harnessed in ways I'd never imagined.

RUN SIX

2001–2002 Season

6th Place – US Open, Slopestyle – 2002

2nd Place – World Championships, Big Air – 2002

RUN SEVEN

'A man would reap very little benefit by his travels, if he made them only in his closet.'

– Philip Dormer Stanhope, Earl of Chesterfield

2003 saw mum Abi and I return to Utah for another winter. We rented the basement of Mitch and Katie Nelson's house. They were the sweetest couple and so much fun. Mitch was a pro snowboarder at the time and I really looked up to him. At the end of the season though, it was clear it was time to find me some permanent accommodation. Mitch was a valuable resource as he moonlighted as a real estate agent; however, it was mum who pulled out all the stops to secure me a home. My age and my status as a 'resident alien' in the US made the task of buying property outlandishly difficult. Eventually her relentless hard work paid off and I was the proud owner of a two-bedroom apartment in Salt Lake City. I was over the moon. I finally had a place of my own where could keep all my belongings.

While Rowe didn't take too many falls on the university ski team that season, she did manage to fall in love. (Rowe insists that she in fact 'rose' in love.) Rise or fall Rowena met Rob who, while he was finishing his pre-medical school courses, had volunteered to be an athletic trainer for her team. They were married in 2003 in Logan, Utah where Rob was born and raised. I was so happy for her; it was a wonderful time of her life. Rowe and Rob purchased a little house and renovated it together during the university vacation. Rob went on to do a PhD in Kinesiology. He is now an assistant professor in the Sports Science School at Brigham Young University in Provo, Utah.

In 2004, I had to get ready to sit my final high school exams, the Higher School Certificate, back in Australia. This was particularly tough as I had such restricted time to do school work. Before the final exams I had six weeks straight to study. Mum tutored me in English and history and I engaged external tutors for mathematics and science. Under the circumstances, I was happy with my results. My UAI (university admission index) was high enough to qualify for various university courses and, as I wanted to attend university at some stage, I was very pleased. For each of us to have our HSC was one of the very important reasons Mum travelled with us.

At this stage I was working without a coach. I just rode with friends, and with the Roxy team. I was pushing myself, trying out new things, and watching carefully what everyone else was doing. I didn't have a set training routine. I had an idea of what I wanted to accomplish and I worked away at it. I would break down the moves and ask myself questions about them. Once you get to a certain point, you understand your own body and what it is doing. You can feel it, even if you can't see it. It's a highly attuned muscle memory. Benny has this mantra I love and borrow: "I become better with every touch of the snow." I was (and am) constantly cultivating a greater connection between myself, my snowboard and the snow. I would challenge myself every day. And every day I was on the mountain, I was getting better.

Around this time Ben and I discussed working together. He had spent the previous year on the Australian Olympic Winter Institute team, which hadn't proved such a great fit. It had been years since we had really ridden together so we decided to spend some time in New Zealand to see what would happen. Ben is an expressive snowboarder and loves it with a passion. He is obsessed with technique and loves smooth flowing lines. We started training at Snow Park in their half pipe. We weren't old enough to rent a car so Dad took some days off work (which was rare) and came over to drive us up to the mountain every day. It was special to be able to spend that sort of time with dad and he loved it too. That period in New Zealand showed us that we worked well together. It was quickly clear to me that he was really going to be able to add something to my riding. Ben is a really active rider, not just someone who sits on the sidelines. While coaching someone through a trick, Ben has to break it down and analyze it himself before he can verbally describe it. This part of his practice is what makes him one of the best riders I know. He has an amazing eye for detail and he's original. He's great at working out interesting trick combinations for slopestyle and pipe.

Ben's vision was for me to push boundaries. I remember clearly the day he asked me: "Why do you want to learn the tricks that all the women are doing? They are all doing the same thing, Torah." He started teaching me some variations of tricks that guys were doing, and some that guys weren't doing. We worked a lot on riding switch (riding backwards). We went way back to basics to learn these different tricks and rotations. We worked on switch front side (cab 180, cab 720) and switch backside (that's the hardest rotation in the half pipe), and switch backside 360s progressing to 720s. Usually I am a goofy rider, which means I lead (and perform tricks) with my right foot. Riding switch meant leading with my left foot. Not many women were riding switch. All the other women were doing front side

900s. However, Brights tend never do what everybody else is doing. I had to relearn a lot but Ben wasn't fazed. We just went and rode the mountain switch until I was comfortable to take it to the transition of the half pipe. That's how I had learned to snowboard right from the start, by riding the mountain. If you can ride switch on the jumps and in the half pipe, it really opens up possibilities for creativity in your runs. There are four ways to spin, plus two more in the half pipe including alley-oop, so why not use them all? I was really excited about this new phase. It was hard work but things were beginning to click. Ben and I had a wonderful creative relationship.

At that time I also met Sarah Burke, a freestyle skier, in Whistler, Canada. Sarah was an icon of the sport and had been incredibly instrumental in getting ski half pipe into the Olympic program. She was the first woman to land a 720, then a 900, then a 1080-degree spin in competition. She was awesome. The top women in snow sports are really motivated and very good at what they do. They are some of the hardest working people I know. Talent is needed but work ethic is what's really required. That said though, you can't keep going hour after hour or you will burn out. It's about working smartly and using the time that you have wisely. I am very focused. I always want to do my best. Snowboarding is not like working a swimming pool or a track. The conditions are changing constantly. You have to be aware mentally or physically whether it's the right time to push yourself or not. Some days you will just ride, and some days you might try three tricks at once. However, overall it is a slow and considered journey. I don't go six to eight feet out of the pipe while I am learning new tricks. Back then the walls were 18 feet; now they are 22 feet high. However high the walls, when you fall, it does kinda' hurt.

During the winter of 2004–2005, our main focus was to qualify for the 2006 Winter Olympics, which were to be held in Torino, in Italy. This meant I had to be on the Federation of Skiing and Snowboarding circuit and earn enough points to get a place in the team. I was placing well and finished runner up FIS Half Pipe Tour Champion. The next competitions I needed to attend were two world cups in Bardonecchia in the Italian Alps in February 2005. It was so exciting to work with Ben on this campaign. I came third in both of those events, which meant that I had passed my Olympic qualifications and I was on the team. I was so excited to compete in my first Olympics. On the Australian half pipe team that year were Ben Mates, Mitch Allen, Andrew Burton, Holly Crawford and I – only five of us.

Snowboarders have felt for a long time that we don't want to be governed by the skiing federation. We still want to be part of the Olympics but we want our own qualification system, one that is better for our sport and governed by snowboarders. It was (and remains) a catch-22 situation. I needed my sponsorship to continue as it was my living but, on the other hand, the Olympics is the biggest platform for our sport that we have. I wanted the chance to compete. Thankfully I had scored enough FIS points from the two world cups. I was able to turn my attention to the professional circuit for the rest of the winter and meet all my sponsorship obligations.

I competed in half pipe and slopestyle, and in both events I was getting great results. I had taken multiple podium places in the half pipe events and was not far behind in the slopestyle. In 2005, Ben and I were invited to Norway to the Arctic Challenge put on by Terje Håkonsen. In those days it was an invite only event and was a huge honour to be invited. It was a quarter pipe contest, which means you perform the same tricks as you would in the half pipe, you just don't have another wall to go up on the other side. I was doing McTwists, one of my favorite tricks, about 4.5

meters out from the quarter pipe, and airs that were 5.5 meters out. This is one of the only times I that I have seen footage of myself and even I was impressed. At that point I was just working hard to stand out from the pack and to develop a technical run that would set me apart. All my hard work seemed to be paying off and I was growing more and more confident in my riding ability.

2003–2004 Season

5th Place – Grand Prix, Superpipe – 2003

2nd Place – FIS World Cup, Canada, Superpipe – 2003

4th Place – FIS World Cup, Chile, Superpipe – 2003

5th Place – Quiksilver Roxy Slopestyle Pro – 2003

6th Place – US Open, Superpipe – 2004

9th Place – US Open, Slopestyle – 2004

3rd Place – Roxy Chicken Jam, Slopestyle – 2004

1st Place – FIS World Cup, Superpipe – 2004

6th Place – The Honda Session, Slopestyle – 2004

4th Place – The Honda Session, Rail Jam – 2004

2nd Place – FIS World Cup, Superpipe – 2004

2nd Place – WSR, Superpipe – 2004

2nd Place – FIS World Cup, Superpipe – 2004

2004–2005 Season

4th Place – World Superpipe Championships– 2005

2nd Place – US Open, Superpipe – 2005

7th Place – US Open, Slopestyle – 2005

3rd Place – FIS World Cup, Superpipe X 2 – 2005

10th Place – Winter X Games, Slopestyle – 2005

4th Place – Winter X Games, Superpipe – 2005

RUN SEVEN

1st Place – Nippon Open, Superpipe – 2005

1st Place – Arctic Challenge, Quarterpipe – 2005

4th Place – Roxy Chicken Jam, Slopestyle – 2005

RUN EIGHT

'The only way to discover the limits of the possible is to go beyond them into the impossible.'
– Arthur C. Clarke

Circe Wallace left IMS Sport in 2005 and I changed to management in Australia. Mark Jones became my wonderfully caring and supportive agent for the next four years. Once again I was very grateful for the wonderful people in my life.

The 2006 Torino Olympics were creeping closer so in June 2005, Ben and I made our way to Mammoth Mountain, California, for a spring training camp. We were working on switch backside tricks again. We spent a couple of weeks riding jumps, the half pipe and the mountain. Training was going well and the results were encouraging, but there was something troubling me. In September 2005, Ben and I travelled to New Zealand to continue training. I felt a little off and I kept calling mum to see what she thought. I had very uncomfortable pain in my abdomen. At the end of October I came home to Australia for some work. One morning during a shoot I felt terrible. As soon as I got back at the hotel with mum, I cancelled the afternoon session. Mum whisked me off to a local doctor who diagnosed me with appendicitis. I was admitted to hospital the next day. I was under the knife for three hours. Mum told me she had been really worried because it was meant to be a one-hour procedure. I was really grateful that the surgeon had been made aware of my snowboarding career. The procedure had taken so long because my surgeon took special care cutting my appendix out bit by bit because he didn't want to weaken my stomach muscles. Core muscles are really very important for me. I was very lucky. In November I went back to the US. I was well enough to ride by December and continue training.

We spent December 2005 and January 2006 training in Breckenridge, Colorado. We would hike the pipe all day long. It was windy and the light was flat, but Ben made me ride in all possible weather conditions. Some days we would have to scrape out the windblown snow in the half pipe and groom it ourselves with our boards. Many times we were the only ones out there. From Breckenridge we drove two hours to Aspen Colorado to compete in the X Games. It's a big annual sports event in the US hosted by the American sports broadcaster, ESPN. It's the holy grail of extreme sports. I rode that pipe to a silver medal. This was my first time on a podium in the X Games. I had never felt better. I had tested my recovering body and the tricks that Ben and I had been working on. I knew we were right on track for the approaching Olympics. I went back to Salt Lake City to refresh and then we jumped on a plane to Italy for my first Olympics representing Australia. I was competing in just one event, the half pipe. It was the only snowboarding Olympic freestyle event at the time.

The only pieces of gear I could bring to the Olympics were goggles, boots, bindings and my board. The rest of my outfit for the Olympics would be the Australian team uniform. So Roxy offered me the opportunity to design my own pair of goggles. They asked me what I wanted on the strap. I did what any rational person would do and asked for diamonds.

I was denied my request but offered the next best thing; Swarovski crystals. It was wonderful. I felt like a glam-rock snow goddess. From this grew my signature line, now called 'Bright Edition'. The boards are not just artistically conceived by me, they're also technically designed and tested by me. The cool thing about purchasing a Roxy board is that what you buy is exactly what I ride. Designing the clothing is particularly fun for me as I can somewhat dictate the trends for the coming winter.

We found accommodation in the mountain village. All the venues were spread out around Torino, which meant that we were separated from the Olympic Village. This was disappointing as the opening ceremony was too far away from where we were staying to feasibly attend. I needed to train the next day. Those who did go to the opening ceremony got back at about three in the morning. I was very sad to miss it, but I was glad that I had conserved my energy for the competition.

During the finals I took a fall. On my first run on the first hit, mid backside 360, my left shoulder partially dislocated. It was a feeling I had never felt before, so I lost my composure in the air. When I fell, I think the shoulder must have gone back into place. I did not quite know what had happened. I remember my fingers feeling numb and tingly. It was very painful. The team doctor came running to see if I was okay. The shoulder was looked at but as it was back in place there was nothing that could be done. I was offered some pain relief but declined. I had another run to do.

I readied myself to try again. I started with a backside 360 into switch backside 540, then a switch front side 720, followed by a front side indy, into a backside Japan and I ended with an air-to-fakie tail. I landed a pretty cool run. I was satisfied. I remember a shirt-less cheer team with my name painted on their chests erupted in ecstatic joy. I laughed as I waited for my results to come through. Half pipe, being a judged sport is quite subjective. I was placed fifth. Hannah Teter, Gretchen Bleiler and Kjersti Buaas took the event. Friends firmly believed I was under scored. Their theory was my run was so different and so new that some of the judges just didn't know what to do with it. However, as usual I wasn't worried about winning, I was just pleased I had managed to put down a run I was proud of. That afternoon, when I arrived back in the village, a USA team coach prophetically told me: "Don't worry, you're going to win a lot of events with that run."

I won every half pipe event I entered for the rest of that season. I took first place in the Vans Cup Superpipe and the World Superpipe Championships and the US Open. I also continued my slopestyle events, and came tenth in the US Open, and fourth at the following X Games. It was a great season. I'd found my distinctive style, the professional circuit liked what I was doing and most importantly, so did I.

In January 2007 back at the X Games in Aspen I won gold. I was overwhelmed, and all my Roxy teammates were so happy for me. It was all happening. I was a competitive machine. My life consisted of event after event, after event. Goggles, helmet, boots, board, tickets, passport, money, jackets, bags. Check in, check out. Train, sleep, compete. Train, sleep, compete. US, Europe, Japan, New Zealand. Supported by Ben, I was feeling secure in my world and in my skills. I was on a fantastic rollercoaster; I felt so lucky to be alive and in my position. By the end of the season I was crowned 2007 TTR World Champion and Burton Global Open Champion, which was huge. Shaun White was the male champion that year.

I was filming for NBC for an X Games piece and all of a sudden I thought: "I am going to do a switch backside 720" (a higher rotation trick than I had ever done before). It worked. I was able to incorporate that into my repertoire from then on. I won the Nippon Open, the Superpipe World Championships in Park City, the Roxy Chicken Jam. At the prestigious US Open Snowboarding Championships, I podiumed on half pipe and slopestyle. The best part was that Rowe could watch me compete as it was close to where she was living at the time.

2007 was also the year Scotty James, a 13-year-old Australian snowboarder, arrived on the scene. Ben smelt that he was really talented and took him on as an athlete. From then on Ben, Scotty and I travelled around to all the events together. We called ourselves the three musketeers. We had so much fun. It was nice for Ben and I to have someone else in the mix; it diversified our dynamic. Scotty became like a little brother (he definitely knew how to irritate me) and we treated him just like he was part of our family. Scotty was introduced to, and was seen by, all the right people who were influencers in the industry. He was Junior European Open Champion in slopestyle and half pipe. He was one of the best juniors in the world.

Roxy was getting a ski program together so naturally they wanted Sarah Burke. As we now had a lot of work together on catalogue shoots, action shoots and were required to represent Roxy at all sorts of events and functions, we had the time to become very close friends. Sarah and I were both competing in the half pipe and slopestyle. I was a huge fan of her work. She was an amazing freestyle skier. She was also an amazing person. She had a fabulous intellect and wit, a ridiculous (and wonderful) sense of fun, she was smart and ballsy and sassy and a total badass. I loved her.

While snowboarding is a really social sport and I am incredibly lucky to know and work with countless great people, it can also be quite an isolating lifestyle. I'm always on the move, so it's hard to really nourish the relationships I have. So many wonderful people in my life put up with me being an absent or long-distance friend. Sarah and I were afforded something rare and special because we could spend so much time together. I am forever grateful I had the time to dance and goof around and party with Sarah, as well as work really hard together. I believe that friendships are our most important relationships. They have a special hue of longevity, trust, love, affection, tolerance and kindness that is quite unique. It's different to romantic and familial relationships (which obviously I'm equally invested in) and I'm so lucky I was able to experience all those things with Sarah.

The next three years were heavy competitive years. I competed in back-to-back events in New Zealand, North America and Japan. We were always on the road, always preparing for the next event. Our season was set. Gone were the days of shredding with no fixed plans. I knew exactly where I was going to be for the next 12 months. Shoots would pop up and we would have to fit them into the schedule. I was only back in Australia for the winter to fulfil obligations and train. It all paid off though, in 2007 I won the Global Open Series again. I was on top of the world and at the top of my game. Ben and I were working really well, and we had our eyes firmly on the Vancouver Olympics in 2010.

2005–2006 Season

4th Place – Roxy Chicken Jam, Slopestyle – 2005

1st Place – Arctic Challenge, Quarterpipe – 2005

1st Place – US Open, Superpipe – 2006

10th Place – US Open. Slopestyle – 2006

1st Place – Vans Cup, Superpipe – 2006

1st Place – World Superpipe Championships, Superpipe – 2006

5th Place – Winter Olympics, Superpipe – 2006

10th Place Overall – TTR World Snowboard Tour Year End Ranking – 2006

RUN EIGHT

Silver Medal – Winter X Games, Superpipe – 2006

4th Place – X Games, Slopestyle – 2006

2006–2007 Season

4th Place – Roxy Chicken Jam, Slopestyle – 2006

8th Place – Burton Open New Zealand, Superpipe – 2006

2nd Place – Roxy Chicken Jam, Superpipe – 2007

3rd Place – Roxy Chicken Jam, Slopestyle – 2007

Gold Medal – Winter X Games, Superpipe – 2007

9th Place – Winter X Games, Slopestyle – 2007

1st Place – Nippon Open, Superpipe – 2007

6th Place – Nippon Open, Slopestyle – 2007

4th Place – Chevrolet Grand Prix, Superpipe – 2007

1st Place – World Superpipe Championships, Superpipe – 2007

2nd Place – US Open, Slopestyle – 2007

3rd Place – US Open, Superpipe – 2007

1st Place – TTR World Snowboard Championship – 2007

1st Place – Burton Global Open Series Championship – 2007

2007–2008 Season

4th Place – Burton New Zealand Open, Slopestyle – 2007

1st Place – Burton New Zealand Open, Superpipe – 2007

1st Place – US Open, Superpipe – 2008

1st Place – Burton Global Open Series Championship – 2008

2nd Place – Roxy Chicken Jam, Superpipe – 2008

7th Place – Roxy Chicken Jam, Slopestyle – 2008

1st Place – World Superpipe Championships, Superpipe – 2008

1st Place – Nippon Open, Superpipe – 2008

RUN EIGHT

Silver Medal – Winter X Games, Superpipe – 2008

2nd Place – Burton European Open, Superpipe – 2008

9th Place – Burton European Open, Slopestyle – 2008

RUN NINE

'Go put your creed into your deed.'

– Ralph Waldo Emerson

Jake Welch is a snowboarder. He makes movies like the ones I used to watch as a young girl in Australia. He's most interested in both backcountry and street snowboarding. In backcountry snowboarding the goal is to find massive lines, natural transitions in landings and to build (and hit) jumps. The street scene is concerned with discovering snow-covered cities on the board. They seek out interesting features to snowboard. They ride things like handrails with stairs below or they find ledges to grind. It's creative, experimental, explorative and exciting.

I (re)met Jake at a soccer match in October 2008, before the start of the northern winter. We had actually met a year prior but didn't really click. People often suggested to me we'd be a good fit and I'd scoff. I didn't think Jake was my type at all. I don't want to sound clichéd, but it was certainly 'something' at first (second) sight. He absolutely charmed me. We had an amazing chemistry. We were connected. I had plans to visit Hawaii with a group of friends and Jake and his friend Brock ended up joining us. The big island was majestic and I had such a wonderful holiday getting to know him.

RUN NINE

While we were in Hawaii, Jake invited me to join him on his family vacation in Mexico. Hasty I know. I was in two minds about accepting the invitation but my friends encouraged me to go. They said it was an opportunity to get to know him better. Jake is the youngest of eight kids most of whom were going to be there. I was more than a little daunted, but I took the plunge, and went straight from Hawaii to Mexico. I was really glad I went. I liked his family. They were very welcoming and I had a ball. We played lots of games on the beach, got sunburnt and shared lots of gorgeous Mexican meals. Jake wanted to have the 'determine the relationship' talk on the way back. I thought he was very bold, but then I had just crashed his family holiday. I agreed to dating exclusively.

I'd had plenty of boyfriends but I'd never felt like this about anyone before. I deeply appreciated our friendship. We lived in each other's pockets. We liked all the same things. We kept active together, enjoyed nice food together and played together. I'm a big romantic. I blindfolded him once and took him to the planetarium so we could watch the stars. We shared an amazing summer; we were getting along so well he even suggested we marry then (three months in). I thought he was joking.

While my heart was getting a feel for the fall it was setting itself up for, I also was having a lot of problems with my shoulder. I had shoulder subluxations. It would pop out mid-event, often mid-run. I would fall and just lay there, screaming and waiting for it to go back in. Then I would get up and do another run. It didn't confine itself to half pipe cameos either. It would pop out in the strangest of situations. I remember being on Manly Beach with my buddy Tom Coles chatting away and all of a sudden I started to scream. He couldn't work out what was wrong and thought he'd stumbled onto the set of *Psycho Beach Party*. It was becoming a big problem. I saw many doctors about it and they would tell me that, if I continued with physiotherapy and kept strengthening it, it would be okay. I did my best to put it out of my mind and concentrate on my work but it continued to plague me.

My shoulder was constantly strapped and the strengthening exercises weren't doing enough to stabilize it. At the last competition of the northern 2009 winter I was riding with Benny and Scotty James and I caught a toe edge on the landing of a jump. I landed straight on my stomach and face. The impact on my shoulder made it drop down and backwards. I was screaming with pain and frustration. This was not what I wanted to be happening a year out from the Olympics. However I couldn't help but find the whole business terribly symbolic. The shoulder is the most movable joint in the body with the poorest support and I was shouldering a lot of different expectations on my failing frame.

Salt Lake City happens to be home of one of the best known shoulder surgeons in the world. I made an appointment with Dr Metcalf and had arthroscopic surgery three weeks later. He had to reattach the labrum ligament to the bone. I spent five months in recovery from April to September 2009 during the northern summer. The timing was good, it wasn't going to ruin any major competitions for me, but the rehab was extremely exhausting. In a bizarre twist of synchronicity, Jake and I had shoulder surgery at the same time. We were even operated on by the same doctor. This meant we did our many months of shoulder rehab together which was some consolation.

Competing drains you on a physical and emotional level but rehab taught me a whole new meaning of hard work. Until that point, I had been one of the biggest medal hopes for Australia at the 2010 Vancouver Olympics. News spread about my surgery and people began to speculate that I was 'out with a shoulder'. I could very well have been if I wasn't so stubbornly invested. I was in a sling for about three weeks then I attended a rehab clinic in Salt Lake every day for two hours of physical therapy. I couldn't lift my arm at all and so I worked tirelessly on getting movement back. I needed to keep fit but I couldn't run or jump. I got creative with my fitness regime and enrolled in ballet bar classes. Ballet was perfect as it's all about lower body strength and had little focus on arms (or shoulders). Dancers are amongst some of the strongest athletes in the world.

Injury is an almost non-negotiable part of an athlete's job description. We push our bodies to their limits so there are bound to be times they give out. I am very grateful to have a sponsor who supports me in sickness and in health. They have had the foresight to allow me time to recover when I need to. A career is about longevity so in the long run five months was nothing. The operation came at a good time too. It would be one thing to miss the northern winter, but to miss the southern wasn't so bad.

By August 2009, I was in Australia working with a trainer. I was now able to use my arm and was building strength. I was busy exercising twice a day and doing a lot of promotional work but I could not wait to get back on the snow. In September I was finally given the okay and we headed to New Zealand. I eased gently into my post surgery riding. I got my feet back under me by cruising the mountain. The five months off snow had been the longest I had ever had.

My first day in the half pipe didn't go super well. I attempted a McTwist but took off too early and landed on the deck of the half pipe, bouncing 22ft into the flats. I was so frustrated. Usually I brush myself off and try again but this time I couldn't. I took off to the side of the mountain, lay on the base of my snowboard with my hood over my head and tried to breathe through my crying.

A few days later I jumped back on the horse, and worked through the barriers that had come from so much time off snow. Tricks that were once so easy to me had to be completely re-learned. I showed up ready to re-learn them though. It was quite an amazing experience rebuilding my strength and repertoire. Before long my muscles had recovered their memories and my trickery was instinctual once more. Towards the end of that camp Ben was prepping me through the beginner moves of another trick when he turned to me and said, "Okay this is it. We are going to do a double crippler." A trick, at that stage, no female snowboarders were performing. Ben believed I could do it. I had complete faith in Ben so I said, "if you say I'm ready, I'm ready." I had watched Shaun White do it plenty of times. Shaun rides natural though and I am a goofy footer. Like I've said before, I like to see a trick in my head before I try it and I wanted to see what it looked like goofy. So I took a video of Shaun and watched it in front of a mirror. I knew what to do.

I had learned a double back flip into the powder a few years prior and we figured it was something we could now work on in the half pipe. The double backflip is a similar rotation as a double crippler but it's different in the pipe because of the vert you take off on and the transition you have to land on. We practiced the move into an airbag, to make sure that I was getting the rotation. Ben talked me through what I needed to think at each step of the trick. I listened, taking it all in. I was eager to try what no woman had yet done in the pipe. I dropped down into the pipe across the flat bottom and initiated for the double crippler. I made the rotation but did not quite stick the landing. I had to walk away from that spring camp without landing the trick, but I was so happy that I had done the hardest part, to try it.

Jake had more time up his sleeve than I did during the southern winters and would join me for periods of time. Jake arrived in New Zealand with a ring and proposed. He made some theatre out of it, we were panning for gold and he slipped the ring into my pan. It was very cute and thoughtful and romantic and I got swept up in the moment, in the cultural script, I said yes.

I kept it a secret for a long time. I didn't want to tell anyone. This should have been a warning signal. It was. I pushed my doubts aside. Ben was the first person I told. He pretended he was happy for me. Later I learned he was far from it. Next I told the James' (we were living at Scotty James' family house in New Zealand), but they didn't believe me. Mum, dad and my manager Mark Jones were the next to hear. They politely said they were happy I was a woman making my own choices. Jake wanted to get married in December. There was no way that I was giving much thought to a wedding two months before the Olympics. I put the engagement out of my head. I was happy to get back to the US, and get stuck into riding and training as I prepared for the northern winter and the coming Olympic Games.

2008–2009 Season

10th Place – Winter X Games, Slopestyle – 2008

1st Place – Burton US Open Snowboarding Championships, Superpipe – 2009

4th Place – Burton US Open Snowboarding Championships, Slopestyle – 2009

1st Place – Winter Dew Tour Toyota Championship, Superpipe – 2009

5th Place – Winter Dew Tour, Slopestyle – 2009

6th Place – FIS World Cup 08/09, Superpipe – 2009

6th Place – FIS World Cup 08/09, Superpipe – 2009

Gold Medal – Winter X Games, Superpipe – 2009

RUN TEN

'We never know how high we are
Till we are called to rise;
And then, if we are true to plan,
Our statures touch the skies.'
– Emily Dickinson

In December 2009 I decided to change my representation back to Circe when she became part of Wasserman Media Group, based in California. These sort of business decisions can certainly be heart wrenching. I value my relationships and I'm invested in unconditional love and gratitude. I was sorry to part ways with Mark but I wanted American action sport representation again and I had a long history with Circe. I headed to the US to start preparing for the Vancouver Olympics.

There was one spot already secured on the Australian Olympic team for the women's snowboard half pipe competition. Holly Crawford had earned the spot, but as the bylaw stipulates, because of my previous year's results, the spot was technically mine. I decided to leave the spot as Holly's and earn another spot for Australia. I needed some more time on snow anyway and a little competition experience post shoulder surgery was not a bad idea. I jumped on a plane to Saas-Fee in Switzerland in November to compete in the World Cup.

Saas-Fee is on top of a glacier and is quite literally an ice pipe. While half pipes have to be solid, they should be snow. There was no traction for the edge of the board to grab on. It was definitely not an ideal pipe, but it served its purpose. I won the event at Saas-Fee and I went home with FIS points and another spot for Australia. Now Holly and I would both compete at the Vancouver games. For the Americans, it was a completely different story. They hadn't decided on their team yet and they had heaps of great riders wanting their four spots. The US team had four or five qualifying events for their team selection. It would be a struggle and the American riders would have to be in all the events right up to the games.

From Switzerland, Ben and I jumped on a plane back to the US to Copper Mountain Colorado and Breckenridge to resume work on the double crippler. It was a really intense period of training. National teams from many different countries were there to get their runs together for the coming events. There were six people in the pipe at any given time. I had attempted the double crippler about four or five times and I was getting closer to properly landing it but the crowded pipe was stressful and I told Ben I was losing my nerve. Ben uncharacteristically lashed out at me and barked: "You need to be doing 20 of these a day." He had never talked to me like that before. We always listened and acted on the warning signs to prevent injury. When you push past those signs, that's when you get hurt. I stuck to my guns and made it clear I was done for the day on that trick.

The next day we were back at the pipe, working again. When you're a pipe jock it can feel like *Groundhog Day*. The same thing, the same tricks, over and over again. Once I warmed up, I was back working on the double crippler. Coming in after the second rotation I just didn't have the right axis and I came in square to the pipe. I smashed my chin, chipped my teeth and my jaw was out. I had neck and shoulder pain as well. Everything else was possible to mend, except my teeth. I needed to fly back to Salt Lake City to go to the dentist and my chiropractor Dr Buhler.

The dentist fixed me up and with the help of Dr Buhler I recovered from my other injuries. I was glad to be riding my home mountain of Park City and I had my favorite physiotherapist, Jess Cunningham, with me. On my first day back riding, I lost my switch backside 720. I just couldn't seem to do it consistently. This didn't bode well. Switch backside 720 was a key trick for my Olympic run. Now I can appreciate that when you lose touch with a trick it's actually an exciting moment. It's an opportunity to push yourself in a different direction. I didn't see it like that though. I wanted the run I'd worked hard on for so long. I drove myself too hard to get it back and I suffered my first concussion for the season. I landed a trick slightly heel-heavy and fell backwards. My head bounced so hard on the bottom of the pipe I suffered whiplash and I was unconscious for a short time. Jess, my physiotherapist, and Jeremy Cooper from Park City came running up the middle of the pipe to me. It was such a blessing that Jess was there to help manage the situation when I came to. It was new territory for us.

I had to rest my brain and keep a close eye on my symptoms for two weeks. I took time off to recover properly even though there was an enormous amount to do. Jess lined me up for a multitude of tests. The most important one with concussion is called a CogSport test. It uses computerised tests to assess a baseline set of criteria for your brain, to see how it is working. It is something you can revisit to compare your functions if you are ever injured. The aim is to ensure that athletes return to action when they are safe to do so. Unfortunately I did not have a baseline before I hit my head. We were working blind. Jess gave me balance exercises and told me I was to stop if any symptoms came on. We did gentle exercises until she felt

I was ready to get back on snow.

Jake told me one evening that my parents were planning on coming over for the Olympics in Vancouver. I immediately rang mum. "Please don't come" I begged her. My reasoning was that anything could happen, I might not be well enough to compete, or it could just end up like it had in Italy. I didn't want the pressure of them watching me and spending all the money to get there. Mum promised me she and dad wouldn't come. I believed her and felt great relief.

In late January, Ben and I made our way to the X Games in Aspen. It's the biggest event of the year and sponsors expect you to be there. On the first training day I mishandled a trick and landed quite flat in the transition. This caused me to fall back and I hit my head just a little bit. We were nervous about this because I was just back from two weeks recovery. We went to look at my CogSport reading and it was fine. I pushed it aerobically in the gym for the next few days to make sure I was okay. I was cleared to go back on the last training day for X Games.

I hit the pipe and was working into some of my trickery. I did a crippler, a trick I could usually do in my sleep. I fell heel-heavy again and hit my head. This time I was concussed. I stood up and slid down to the bottom of the pipe. People came to me, unbuckled my board and took my helmet off. My head was rolling back. I was awake but I wasn't. I was talking gibberish. The medical staff got me out of the pipe quickly. My head was propped up only by the car window as they drove me to the medical room. When we arrived I was just becoming aware of where I was as the medical staff asked if I was ready to sit up. I tried and burst into tears. I was really freaked out. So was Ben. He'd never seen me like this before. The medical staff explained that I had just sat up too early. While this was going on, Ben rang dad and told him, "We're not going to go to Vancouver.

It's pointless. The way things are at the moment, we're just about a write off."

No more X Games for me. I went back to the house where we were staying and went straight to bed. I was so dizzy, I felt seasick. The papers in Australia went ballistic. The accident just two weeks out from start of the Vancouver Winter Olympics sparked immediate concerns back home about whether I would compete. I was very low in energy but I wanted to let people know that Australia still had a chance with me. I did an interview with Channel Nine and said I was fine. I lied. I wasn't fine.

I ventured back to Salt Lake City with Jess and Ben in tow looking after me. The recommended recovery strategy was to stay in a dark room with minimal stimulation. That's what I did. But I couldn't shut my brain down. I was visualizing the run I wanted to do in Vancouver and playing it over and over like a video in my mind. Ben flew a pregnant Rowe with little Syd over to me to help me through this time. He knew I needed my sister. When I heard their voices I just fell to my knees. I cried and gave my nephew a hug. I was overwhelmed with love and gratitude. Ben took Rowe into the next room. When she asked what my chances were of making it to the Olympics he replied bluntly, "We're fucked."

I had just over two weeks to recover. My chiropractor, Dr Craig Buhler who pioneered muscle activation therapy, examined me. He inserted a small balloon about the size of a little finger into my nasal passages and inflated it. It reset that cranial mechanism and my balance was better instantly. Within a week I was back on my feet. It was remarkable. I began working on balance and aerobics. Every day I tested my limits and was slowly seeing progress with my symptoms.

Ben and I flew out from Salt Lake City with Scotty James who had qualified at the last minute. Scotty was only 15 at the time and was debuting as Australia's youngest ever Winter Olympian at the 2010 Vancouver

Games. I got on that plane to Vancouver accepting that I may not feel well enough to compete when I got there. I had suffered three head injuries and I wasn't sure what would be possible. We arrived and I went straight into medical examinations. I had a brain scan and was assessed by multiple doctors. There was only one thing I cared about at this stage. I was set on having a real Olympic experience. Not only was I going to attend the opening ceremony this time, I found out the night before the ceremony that I would be carrying the Australian flag. I was honoured and humbled. Whether I made it into the pipe or not, I was leading my country into the Winter Olympic games.

I rented a house for Rowe's family, Craig, and Jake's entourage who had all travelled to support me. When I rang Rob to see if he could pick up the tickets. I thought I heard some familiar voices in the background. "Rob, is that mum in the car with you?" I asked. He pretended the phone was cutting out and hung up. When I arrived at the house, I conducted a reconnaissance mission to see if I could find any signs of mum and dad. Then I asked Rowena if mum and dad were here, she just shot me a wry smile and said: "No, why would you think that?"

Training had been postponed for a few days because of the weather. The organizers needed more time to fix the pipe. On the first day of training, I just took my time feeling out the transition. The half pipe was in a laughable state. The warm conditions and rain had made the snow soft and inconsistent. You were doing well if you could make it across the flat bottom without pancaking in to the walls. On the last night of training, it was the most rideable it had been and I was able to link my run together. I was very happy that I felt good and strong on my snowboard.

The half pipe was a one-day event. It started at 8 am and ran through to 10 pm. I landed the run I had prepared in the qualification round and went straight through to the finals. I had qualified in 1st place. I rested while the semi finals were on. It was a night event, which meant the half pipe was lit by massive floodlights. The snow sparkled and it took me right back to my evening rides in Australia with Adam. I smiled to myself, now I was performing for the world, not just my mates in Cooma. Despite the dramatic triple-concussion lead up, I was at the top of Cypress mountain, and about to compete in the finals of the women's Olympic snowboard half pipe competition.

We were given a bit of time to practice in the pipe before the event. I worked out where the hits were that I needed to back off from with speed so I could safely execute my tricks. It was a little frustrating to have to interrupt the flow of the run to make sure that I was able to stay in control and land the tricks. Part of the show is creating amplitude, but I had to play to the level of the pipe. When I was attempting my switch backside 720, I was over rotating to a 900. This can be a great thing, but it wasn't what I wanted. I had a run in mind and I needed the 720 to position myself for the next trick I had planned. A 900 would change how it ran together. I came off the pipe and went straight to Ben, really startled. All Ben said was "Hey it's funny how that works, isn't it? All that means it that your body is ready to move on to bigger things," he said. "But we want the 720" I responded expectantly. He calmly explained the motion I needed to find instead of what I'd been doing to end up in a 900.

The format of the event is that each finalist does two runs and the best run counts. As I qualified first I was to run last. This meant I ran with full knowledge of how my competitors had performed and how the table looked. Hannah Teter, the 2006 gold medallist, had nailed a clean run and was in first place on a comfortable 42.4. 17-year-old Liu Jiayu held second place on 39.3 and Sophie Rodriguez was third with 34.4. Snowboarding legend and world champion Kelly Clark had taken a fall in her first run and was sitting on 25.6. X Games champion Gretchen Bleiler had also had some trouble with her first run, she had not landed her crippler 720, which had been giving her grief in this particular pipe. Now it was my turn to show the world what I was made of.

I stood at the top of the drop in, strapped my feet to my board and adjusted my goggles. I gave a pound to Ben, slid down on my edge and stopped to get in the zone. I placed my hands on my knees and waited for a smile to arrive on my face. My smile always lets me know I'm ready. I dropped in. First hit, backside 360, into a switch backside 720. I got baulked on the initiation of the trick and fell. The run was over. I slid to the bottom of the pipe, passing the finish line. I was in last place on a score of 5.9 (out of 50). It would all be down to my next run.

I jumped on the back of the snowmobile and rode to the top of the pipe. As I was in last place I would now ride first in the second half of the event. Ben and I quickly talked through the fundamentals of what went wrong. There was a nervous look in Ben's eyes. I gave him a hug and he looked at me and said, "I have supreme confidence in your ability." We knuckled and I slid down into position to collect myself and focus on my final run. My hands went to my knees, I smiled, I dropped in. I went straight into a backside 360, a perfect switch backside 720 (finally), a backside 540, an air-to-fakie and I finished with a cab 720, which felt great. When a trick feels great, it usually looks great too. I saw my board cross the finish line. I did it. I landed a nice, clean run and I was safe. I waited for my score to come through; 45.0. I was in first place.

Hannah Teter was now in second place and Liu Jiayu 3rd. The event was by no means over though. 10 other finalists had their second run to complete. Gretchen was up next; she landed a beautiful front side 900, but sadly left the pipe too early clipping the pipe with her nose on the cab 720. She wasn't going to place. My teammate, Holly Crawford, put down a solid run but was only scored 30.3. Elena Height took a fall on her run and was out of contention. Kelly Clark screamed "you shall love me" into the night air as she dropped in and made a fabulous run. The judges gave her 42.2. She assumed third place nudging Liu Jiayu off of the podium. Ursina Heller took a fall and scored 18.1. Sun Zhifeng made a nice run scoring 33.0. Mercedes Nicoll fell on her front side 5 and wasn't able to improve on her first score. Then Sophie Rodriguez, who had been in 3rd place at half time prepared herself to try and climb back up the ladder. She fell on her first hit attempting a front side 1080. Liu Jiayu, landed a clean run but was scored slightly lower than her first and remained in 4th place. This meant I had a medal. We knew now that Kelly, Hanna and I would be on the podium. However Hanna still had her final run and it would determine whether she or I took home gold. She nailed a good run: method air, front side 900, backside 540, front side 360, cab 720, front side 720. She waited in anticipation while the judges finalized their scores. She scored 39.2. I had the gold.

Ben and I hugged, and then he pointed to the stands and said, "look up there!" Our parents had been hiding in the grandstands the whole time and they'd been hiding in the bathroom closet when I had searched the house. Rowena set them up with a DVD player and pillows and told them, "I don't know how long Torah is going to stay here so get in the closet and don't make a noise." They had obeyed. Dad apparently fell asleep and was snoring loudly. Despite my suspicions, I believed her that they weren't there. It was an incredible surprise to look up and see them in the grandstand, beaming with pride. It was perfect.

I joined Kelly and Hannah for the podium flower ceremony and then

I took a quick congratulatory phone call from Kevin Rudd, the Prime Minister of Australia at the time. After that it was off to doping control. I did not leave the mountain until midnight. I was dropped off at the family house so I could be with everyone. When I woke in the morning I had a deep sense of satisfaction. I was the first Australian snowboarder to achieve a gold medal in the Winter Olympics. And I was bringing home Australia's fourth winter gold ever – Steve Bradbury, Alicia Camplin, Dale Begg-Smith, now mine. Lydia Lassila won gold five days later at Vancouver for aerial skiing so that took our tally to five.

While I maintain that competition results don't define me, in this case, I wanted to win, for myself, for Ben, for my family and for my country. It was like a rock concert at the medal ceremony at VC stadium. It was a little overwhelming. I remember being up on stage and our Australian anthem was playing and I was singing. My lip was twitching I was smiling so hard. It was so surreal. After that there was a huge medal party for me with much glitter and lots of dancing. Circe was there along with all of my Roxy pals.

I couldn't go home to Australia straight away as there was the European X Games to compete in. I was so exhausted. I should have come home and shared it with Australia but I felt like I had to keep competing. I placed second. Roxy threw a massive congratulations party for me at the European X Games. By the end of March, I was free to come home. On arrival at Sydney airport with Circe, there were TV cameras welcoming me. I stayed in Sydney for a while for press and a few meetings. Then it was home to Cooma where the town did an amazing job of putting together celebrations for the local Olympians: Jenny Owens and Ben Sims, Scott Kneller, Jono Brauer, Ramone Cooper and me. Pelican Airways generously flew me along with all my Sydney-based family to Cooma to join in the celebrations. It was a rare treat to see them all, especially my great aunt Angela. The Mayor, along with lots of local kids, greeted us upon landing and I remember the local fire brigade made an impressive water arch to welcome us on our arrival into town. Each athlete was given an old vintage car from the Cooma Car Club and we formed a motorcade through Sharp Street. Mine was a Triumph. Ben, mum, dad and I all sat in the back and waved to the crowds. A large rock was collected from one of the local farm areas and a plaque was created with all local Olympians names on it. Celebrations continued all day.

While home I spoke with Imants Tillers. We had gone to school with his daughters and he had helped Rowe with her Year 12 major artwork. I asked him if he would consider designing the artwork for my next snowboard. Imants' parents emigrated from Latvia after the war and he was born here. He works with famous Aboriginal artist, Michael Nelson Jagamarra. His board graphic was intended as a celebration of Australia's diverse history. It came out beautifully. He also ended up weaving my story into one of his iconic paintings. Letters and words that signify his feelings for my win and my snowy-ways crawl along his 16-panel canvas. I was honored to hear this news and incredibly moved when I saw the work.

It was an immensely special trip home. I felt such warmth from Australia. Everyone was so proud of my achievement and excited for me. It was time though to head back to my other home and finalize my wedding plans. It was not far away now, but for some reason I couldn't really muster adequate enthusiasm for the event. I was worn out. I should have been buzzed but for some reason, that I couldn't quite place, my impending wedding evoked more stress than delight.

RUN TEN

2009–2010 Season

1st Place – FIS World Cup, Superpipe – 2009

Silver Medal – Winter X Games Tignes, Superpipe – 2010

Rider of the Year, Snowboard Magazine – 2010

Gold Medal – Vancouver Winter Olympics, Superpipe – 2010

RUN ELEVEN

'The most common way people give up their power is by thinking they don't have any.'
–Alice Walker

We had planned our big day for June 4, 2010 and it was time to get everything ready. Long days were spent preparing in the lead up and this time was valuable as it bonded our families together. The beautiful secret garden-esque property was stunning with string lighting, white and ivory ribbon, lace and flowers hanging from the trees. And of course, the dance floor was set and ready to be ripped. I had wanted to elope but Jake's family wanted a proper wedding. We were married in a small, intimate, simple and beautiful ceremony in the Salt Lake City Temple. The weather was perfect. My dress was ivory lace. I felt beautiful. It was a wonderful, loving, joyful day but I did experience one flash of doubt. For a split second I knew very clearly I wasn't making the right choice. I loved Jake dearly, don't get me wrong, but part of me always knew we weren't the right fit. It was akin to attempting a trick when your body is warning you not to. I wanted this relationship so badly, but my body was sending me all sorts of signals that I wasn't ready. I drowned out those doubts because I loved him so much but they were immutable. I looked at my soon-to-be-husband across the temple and tried to quell the sinking feeling that flashed momentarily in my soul. I dropped in – I said "I do" and my run with Jake began.

I decided to keep my last name. My reasons for this were purely pragmatic, Bright is the name of my brand. I'm known professionally as Torah Bright and I also have Roxy Bright Edition range to think about. Welch was just never going to have the same punning impact. I firmly believed (and still do) that as women, we don't have to be subsumed into our partner's identity. We can love someone entirely and passionately and still retain who we are. I'd been Torah Bright my whole life; I wasn't about to go changing that.

Sarah Burke was also married that year in September 2010. Sarah and her partner Rory exchanged their vows at Cedar View Estate in Pemberton, British Columbia in Canada. I was sadly unable to attend as I was working in New Zealand at the time. I so wish I'd been there to help then celebrate their love. I've since made a pact with myself that I will never put work in front of an important personal event again.

After my incredibly gruelling schedule in the lead up to the 2010 Olympics, and the several concussions I had suffered, it was recommended that I have a low impact year. I was ready for that. For the oncoming winter 2010–2011 season, I wanted to explore different aspects of snowboarding that I hadn't had a chance to before, especially in the backcountry. I bought a snowmobile and Jake taught me how to drive it. I spent my winter traveling to where the snow was. There was a ton of snow in Utah that year but I also took some great trips to Canada. I didn't compete in any major events but I was still training and working for my sponsors, doing shoots, riding and non-riding. I was still busy.

I had a great crew including Roxy teammate, Erin Comstock, with whom I was filming. Our days would start early; we'd meet at the trail head with sleds in tow as the sun was rising. We would jump on the sleds and find a cool location. Then we'd build our own jumps, manicure them for hours until they were ready to hit, then we'd do our thing. It was also amazing to find natural hits and little poppers. Free riding is an indescribable rush. I had a blast. It was fun to be with my friends and not have the pressure of a major competition. This style of winter was exactly what I needed. Very little pipe and park, just riding powder. However nothing is really ever low-impact. I was challenging myself in a different way on my snowboard. I called it my stoke year, where I brought back the 'stoke factor' into my riding.

Dad rang me up one day and said "Guess what? You've been nominated for an Order of Australia Medal." I was blown away. Jake accompanied me to Government House in Canberra for the reception to receive the medal. Now I am Torah Bright OAM. Mum, dad and Robin came to watch the ceremony. It was a beautiful day in Canberra. The Governor General, Quentin Bryce, awarded the medal to me. She was so lovely, and had something personal to say to everyone that day. I sat in the hall listening to all the speeches about the other medal recipients and heard about their accomplishments. Some people had achieved breakthroughs in the fields of research, science, medicine and were making a real difference to people's lives. I was feeling a little out of place. Quentin Bryce said I was a great role model to young women and that the country had been so proud of me when I won the gold medal. Then she said her grandkids thought she was the coolest getting to meet me. That made me laugh. She was an extraordinary woman and I was so inspired by her grace and warmth.

As I've probably adequately foreshadowed, Jake and I were not experiencing the marital bliss that some newly weds talk about. Of course there were some lovely times, but mostly it was heart-wrenchingly hard.

RUN ELEVEN

There were plenty of red flags towards the end of our engagement, but I would rationalize around in circles until I believed everything was okay. It wasn't okay. Now I was married and miserable. Our relationship needed some serious work. I found us a highly-recommended marriage councillor and Jake and I started couples therapy. I was bewildered that it was so hard so soon but I was committed to doing everything I could to make it work. I threw myself into therapy the same way I threw myself into my snowboarding, with fierce determination. I was convinced both that I loved Jake and that we could save our marriage. In the end we saw three different marriage counsellors.

In 2011 I was named Women's Rider of the Year in the Transworld Magazine Snowboarding Rider Poll Awards, I was voted number one Female Rider of the Year for Snowboarder magazine, I was awarded Female Actions Sports Athlete of the Year at the ESPY Awards and I was a Choice Action Sports Female Nominee at the Teen Choice Awards. That meant a lot of functions, a lot of parties and a lot of dresses. As usual, Sarah and I attended these events together but I didn't have my usual energy. If there was anyone that put a (genuine) smile on my face during that period though it was Sarah. She could occasionally coax me out of the darkness to have fun and laugh and goof around at those events.

That spring I went to Miss Super Park, a big all girls magazine shoot and film event. I was riding with a lot of radical women and hitting incredibly fun features. I should have been having a ball, but I wasn't. I could barely function. I was with all my favorite people and I didn't want to get out of bed. Small things were incredibly hard. To feel this way was new and weird for me. I've always had seemingly infinite resources, and an incredible drive. I'd dried up. I was running on empty and I had no idea why. I should have been full of joy, I'd just had a career defining win, Australia was proud of me and recognizing my achievements, I was having an experimental low-impact year, I had interesting exciting work with Roxy and I'd married a man I adored. Why did I feel so lost?

Female Actions Sports Athlete of the Year – ESPY Awards – 2010

Choice Action Sports Female Nominee, Teen Choice Awards – 2010

#1 Women's Rider of the Year, Transworld Snowboarding Rider Poll Awards – 2011

#1 Female Rider of the Year, Snowboarder Magazine – 2011

Order of Australia for services to sport – 2011

RUN TWELVE

'Life is not easy for any of us. But what of that? We must have perseverance and above all confidence in ourselves. We must believe that we are gifted for something and that this thing, at whatever cost, must be attained.'
– Marie Curie

On my arrival back into Utah for the season I did my best to get in gear for competition but it just wasn't clicking. Small things suddenly were incredibly hard. I found concentration difficult. I was in a fog of uncertainty. I started to question if I was still passionate about snowboarding.

Ben had arrived late to start the season, which was frustrating as I was intending to return to full competition and we had the next Olympics to start preparations for. Ben and I spent a few days on the mountain and I could feel his heart wasn't in it. I asked him what was going on. It all came tumbling out that he wasn't entirely happy coaching. That he loved me and loved the team we made there was no question, but he felt like he wasn't living out his dreams. He wasn't sure what he wanted to do, but he knew he needed some time to work it out. I didn't want him to go but I knew I couldn't stand in his way. With a heavy heart, I began to prepare for a Ben-less winter.

I was putting myself through my paces the next day up at Park City when

RUN TWELVE

I ran into Sarah. I talked to her about my situation and without missing a beat she said: "Don't sweat it Torah. Come and train with Trennan and me." Trennan Paynter was Sarah's coach. I liked him and I loved Sarah, finally something was falling into place. Sarah's gorgeous positivity was just what I needed. I began to thaw a little and find my feet on the mountain again. Sadly though, disaster struck and I didn't get the chance to commence training with them.

On January 10, 2012 we were training in the half pipe when I decided to break for lunch. During lunch I suddenly felt this pang, "Where is Sarah?" Then I saw someone being taken down the mountain by the ski patrol. My heart sank. I had a dreadful feeling it was Sarah. I got up and started running down to the ski patrol. She was surrounded by a group of people and was being resuscitated. Then she was flown to hospital. We were all in shock. I jumped in my car and drove down the mountain. I rang Rowe and our Roxy team manager Amber Stackhouse but could barely choke the words out about what had happened. That night I went to the hospital in Salt Lake City and sat in the waiting room along with many of her loved ones. Her husband Rory was in Whistler and was trying to find the fastest way to get to the hospital. Sarah's vertebral artery had been severed. The doctors decided that they would operate to try to repair the artery. We all had so much hope that she would recover.

I stayed in the hospital as a support for Sarah and her family. We all tried to stay positive for her. After ten of the longest days of my life, we were told that Sarah would not make it. We all said our goodbyes and left her in the hospital with her family. Everyone in the whole industry was rocked to the core over the loss of such an incredible individual. My heart still aches for her husband Rory, her family and her sweet nephews. Sarah was a woman who lived and loved life to its fullest. She was a light.

She touched many hearts and was a soul this world needed so much.

Jake was off filming for the winter and had no plans to come home so I got on a plane to be with Rowe for some emotional support and nephew cuddles. She had just moved to Albuquerque, New Mexico. Everything was a little overwhelming. I felt I didn't deserve life; that I wasn't appreciating what I had. I was angry and thought it was wrong that Sarah was taken from this world. I wished with every fibre of my strength that it had been me. It was good to be with Rowe. I'd not seen her for some time. I'd been so low I'd withdrawn from all of my close relationships aside from Jake.

Despite knowing full well my marriage was difficult, I never really processed that it was the root of my depression. As the winter wore on there was a constant battle being waged inside my head. I was trying to figure out if it was snowboarding that was making me so miserable, or the grief of losing Sarah. Jake suggested it might be due to the multiple concussions I'd sustained in the lead up to Vancouver. I checked myself in for brain scans. Nothing was conclusive. I needed some time to think, to take stock and make some big decisions. I had no interest in being on my snowboard. I was barely keeping my head above water. I thought that maybe it was time to quit. Perhaps Sarah's accident was the universe telling me to stop. I was so conflicted.

I was torn between my obligations as a professional snowboarder and what I also desperately needed, personal time. I knew I wanted to be back on top professionally but mostly because that is where I was expected to be. I realized that wasn't a good enough reason but time waits for nobody and the Winter X Games in Aspen as usual were coming up fast. I decided to go. I felt I needed to be there for Sarah's memorial if nothing else. It was a dangerous decision. I shouldn't have been anywhere near a competition but I am a stubborn woman. Sometimes I think I can do it all. I was expecting too much of myself. I am pleased I was there for Sarah though. All the snowboarders and skiers performed a (physically and emotionally) moving tribute. Those who loved her slowly slipped down the pipe with candles in hand, gently cradling their lights, and their memories.

My schedule continued after the X Games. I had a Roxy team photo shoot and an event in Europe and I also had Ryan and Wade Gardner following me and filming my 'Road to the Olympics' which felt like a big joke. At this point I didn't know if I was going to make it to the games or even if I wanted to. It was totally up to me if I chose to go to Europe for these two events. The last thing anyone wanted was for me to push myself past my limits and get injured. I thought it would be good to keep moving (read: running). The minute you slow down, everything catches up. I wasn't ready to face my grief. I threw myself back into work to distract myself. I usually love being with the Roxy girls. We have such a fun and creative time together, always laughing and playing pranks. I thought that being with fun-loving like-minded girls might pick me up. It didn't but it did remind me how down I was. It forced me to face my denial. When I got to the shoot in Gerlos, I slept alongside my injured roommate, Erin Comstock. The day I arrived she had taken a fall and punctured her lung. We were both hurting over the loss of Sarah. We shared our physical and emotional pain and I realized that I needed to process what was happening. With the blessing of those at Roxy, I left the shoot and flew home. That decision was a massive one for me. I have a deep work ethic. This time though, I put myself before work. Looking back it was a turning point.

I was home alone in my house. I did not reach out to anyone. Jake was away, so I did what I pleased: nothing. I was so broken I did not know where to start healing. So I didn't. I would love to say that I did a lot of soul searching and figured everything out, but the truth is I just binge-watched TV to escape. It felt therapeutic at the time. I drowned my sorrows with copious amounts of Don Draper. Like so many have before me, I immersed myself in art (okay and a bit of trash). I lost and found myself in narratives. I surrendered myself to the heartbeat of storylines. Shows became my therapist, my refuge, my friendship group. Television lived for me so I didn't have to.

RUN THIRTEEN

'Love blurs your vision; but after it recedes, you can see more clearly than ever'
– Margaret Atwood

Ben was working with Danny Davis and was planning on being with him until the 2014 Olympic Games. I happened to be in New Zealand at the same time as Ben and we each expressed interest in working together again. It was a perfect fit in that moment. He was my brother; he cared about me more than he cared about a gold medal. That was exactly what I needed. I needed both emotional support and someone who had the technical skills on the mountain to help me get back to where I needed to be. Ben was the only person on earth who fitted that description. What I needed was a brother-coach, and luckily for me Ben had a renewed interest in coaching right when I needed him most.

I had to sort out my life before November, when my season seriously began. I knew I couldn't go on in the emotional state I was in. Mum arranged for me to see a specialist to whom I will forever be grateful. She had a PhD in psychoanalysis and gave me explanations about the mess I was in and suggestions on how to investigate further and make some choices. It took me a while to absorb, but I realized once and for all that my marriage was making me miserable. Basically what I learned is there are certain personality combinations that make it very difficult to have a successful relationship. When personality types differ so greatly, each other's basic and essential life needs cannot be met. It becomes a struggle to survive. I started to see clearly what I had to do.

I filed for divorce. Two years of therapy with various practitioners had failed. Now I was moving forward with proper knowledge and knew what to do. I was advised by my therapist and attorney that no contact was best for both of us. I met with Jake to let him know what I had decided. From then on, our individual attorneys did the work. It was harsh but essential advice. I knew I'd made the right call. Instead of hating myself and trying desperately to repair a marriage I deep down always knew wasn't right, I chose me. It wasn't easy. I still believed I was in love with him. Letting go was painful and difficult. However the intense relief I felt alongside the grief signalled that this was the right move. The fog that had lurked for so long was lifting and I could clearly see the winter ahead (and what I wanted from it).

The divorce was in full swing by the time I left for Colorado, but I had my new canine friend to cuddle and love, Obi. Rowena encouraged me to get him, and offered her place as his second home when I flew south. I was in luck as my brother-in-law Rob had finished his PhD and they had moved back to live in Utah. Obi is a Cavoodle and yes, he's named after Obi Wan Kenobi from *Star Wars*. The love of an animal is a powerful 'force' and like his namesake, Obi is a great traveller. Wherever we drove, Obi came. Benny, Obi and I set off on our training adventures and my heart was starting to lift.

While we were on the mountain in Colorado, Ben was told by a friend that a wax tech had made the disparaging comment: "The train has left the station and Torah is not on it." When I heard this I just thought: "Oh, people are funny". I don't ever let stuff like that faze me. I knew it was quite the opposite. I'd finally boarded the train. I'd left my marriage along with all my baggage on the platform. I was alive. I was riding like I was a 12-year-old kid again. I had so much excitement about my future. I remembered I *did* love snowboarding. I was back.

RUN FOURTEEN

'Gazing through her chamber window
Sits my souls dear soul:
Looking northward, looking southward,
Looking to the goal,
Looking back without control.'
– Christina Rossetti

Ben pitched me the idea that we could compete in three events at the Sochi Olympics in Russia. Snowboard slopestyle was going to be a new event at the games, obviously I'd compete in the half pipe, and I could also compete in snowboard cross. My first response was 'no way' but I quickly realized it was the exact challenge I needed. I needed to re-discover my true love: snowboarding. I needed to enjoy everything it had to offer. I needed to court the snow again, the devoted lover I'd neglected.

Snowboard cross is a mixture of speed and airtime. It's more race-orientated and requires a different technique than the slopestyle and half pipe. In my mind, half pipe is the most technical event. If you can ride a half pipe well, you can ride anything. That being said, they are all difficult and require different skills. Those skills do take a lot of time to develop properly. Snowboard cross was a serious world. It is the rider against the clock for seatings into the rounds and then six riders fight to be first across the line. Slopestyle and half pipe are judged events and are about personal style. It's a pure self-expression of on a snowboard.

I had a lot of riding to do. I had to put a lot more time on snow if I was to qualify in these three events. The Dew Tour in early December at Breckenridge Colorado was my first competition of the 2012–13 season. I came fourth in the Superpipe. While I didn't podium, everyone agreed, "Whoa, Torah is back." I was riding well, even though I was doing simple tricks. I wasn't doing anything I didn't want to do. At this event and on many occasions that season, I was told I was glowing. This made me happy, as I felt it too. I was in the thick of my divorce and shredding my little heart out. I was recovering, but I was also a new and improved woman regaining her power and strength.

The Grand Prix event at Copper Mountain was a FIS qualifier for the Olympics. It was challenging for me as I was suffering from a particularly bad cold. My body ached. It was typically Colorado cold during the event. It was so cold that our boards, despite being prepped to the nines would not glide on the snow. As usual there was nothing we could do but adapt to the conditions. I was thinking about not competing because I was so sick. I did a few runs in training and had to lie down and rest. Walking and being upright felt hard but yet again I battled through and competed. Regardless of the conditions and the miserable weather, I was loving being on the mountain. I was with my friends and snowboarding. That's all I wanted. Surprisingly, I pulled a couple great runs out and won the event. It was my first win for the season and it meant that I had most likely secured my spot on the Australian Olympic team for half pipe. As long as I stayed in the top 30, I wouldn't need to do any more FIS half pipe events. One event down, two more qualifications to meet.

RUN FOURTEEN

There was also a slopestyle event at this Grand Prix. I wanted to compete so I could start accumulating points. It was terrible weather, with fresh snow on the course, which meant there wasn't enough speed to clear the jumps. A lot of the athletes, including myself, were saying that the event should be postponed. Apparently this was not possible. It was the first time that slopestyle was going to be included in the Games. At these qualifying events, there is a lot of varying skill levels with everyone trying to make the qualification criteria. The coaches felt pressure to deliver good results. There was a lot of talk going on to try and work out the best way to handle the contest. What shocked me was that a lot of coaches were saying, "just send the girls down and get on with it." I got really infuriated about this. Some coaches were not putting safety first and pushing their girls to go, even when several of them didn't want to. Some of the younger girls were saying silly things like "I'll hit the jumps, I'm not scared" even though it was obvious that it was dangerous to send anyone. That day I witnessed what I like to call 'Olympic fever'. I was shocked and disappointed at the way some of my peers and coaches were behaving. It was not the top girls whom I was worried about; it was the less skilled and inexperienced riders that I feared for. We all waited for a bit and the weather cleared. I was so outraged by the shenanigans I'd witnessed that I was not present when it came to my ride. I fell on both runs and ended up in last place. Sadly that event did not help me make the slopestyle qualification for the Games, but luckily I had a few more chances remaining.

Ben's idea of training was to ride all day and ride everything. We rode jumps, rails, pipes and the mountain. The rationale was that this would help me develop the skills on my snowboard that I'd need across the three disciplines. There was nothing to lose and everything to gain. I decided to ride to the beat of my heart. I wasn't going to do tricks that weren't fun for me. It was back to the *Mary Poppins* principle.

Finding the fun in work is easy when you love what you do. Likewise, it's so important that I treat myself with love. I always make sure I am nourished. Eating good food and getting the right amount of sleep is very important for general wellbeing. Because of my upbringing I am mindful of what I eat, but I'm certainly no fanatic. I'm an intuitive eater. I listen to my body and give it what it wants. When I'm training I tend to eat a lot of meat. I eat a fair amount of vegies and greens too and sugar is my vice. I love chocolate. I'm an addict. When I am eating too much I notice a huge difference in my energy levels. When I notice the signs, I have a sugar-free period for a little detox but, just like a true addict, I'm straight back in there after awhile.

I don't drink alcohol. I never have. I suppose to begin with this decision was inflected by my religious upbringing but it's not now. I'm just not interested. My religion afforded me a distance I suppose. I was not culturally indoctrinated to love drinking the way most teenagers in Australia are and with that distance I had the time to make up my own mind. Drinking, in Australia is normalized, we're socialized to believe drinking makes everything more fun; parties, theatre, watching sport, hanging out at the beach, sunshine, romance they're somehow more interesting with a drink in your hand. I've never bought into that, and to be honest, I've seen the darker side of what the drug does to people. How addictive it is. The way it destroys lives. I don't think it's worth romanticising the way people do. It also comes back to that sugar-in-the-car-engine metaphor. I'm really careful about what I put into my body. I don't see the point in poisoning it solely for hedonistic purposes. I've also never needed alcohol to have fun. I've always had a solid group of friends. We dance, we shred, we egg each other on, play pranks, play cards, we throw impromptu parties outside our cars when we're on the road, and fly kites at 3 am. I guess I'll never know, but I'm pretty sure alcohol wouldn't have made any of these things more fun.

I stayed out of Utah for Christmas. Instead of going home to Salt Lake with Rowena, Rob and the nephews, Ben and I stayed in Breckenridge and rode. A Christmas and a birthday shred were just perfect. Ben and I were a double-headed-Christmas-grinch together that year. (To be fair, Ben has always been). We wanted to forget all about it. I didn't want to know about my birthday either, which was unusual for me. Birthdays have always been very special in our family. I turned 26 without celebrating.

The world championships held in a resort called Stoneham in Quebec Canada were another opportunity for me to compete in an FIS slopestyle event. Stoneham is known for being freezing cold. It was minus 35 celsius during our event. I managed to nab a third place in slopestyle. It was possible that my Olympic qualification could be done with this one result but we would have to keep our eyes on the points list to make sure I did not slip out of the top 30. So I had a tentative two of three qualifications at this stage however I had yet to set foot on a snowboard cross track.

The snowboard cross qualification was always the questionable one. I had not been on a track since I was 15. It was a long and uncertain road. I had accepted the possibility I would fail. Because of my crowded competition schedule, my options as to what snowboard cross events I could attend were limited, and even more limited because I had to start from the bottom. I could not just turn up to a World Cup event in snowboard cross and compete. I had not yet accumulated any FIS points. I had one option, which was a tricky one because it fell right at the same time as the X Games. There were two NorAm events which had low-level entry points. However, if I was able to make finals in those two NorAm events, I should have enough points to make it to the World Cup tour.

This was essential for my Olympic qualification. X Games is the highest profile event in action sports, broadcast to millions. I spoke about it with my Roxy Team Manager, Amber Stackhouse. Of course she wanted me to be at X Games and represent the brand but she was okay with whatever I decided. She knew the Olympics were my focus this year. I decided that I was going to compete in both the X Games and the NorAm. It was a little insane but worth a try. Ben and I spent our days on Copper Mountain riding the snowboard cross (SBX) track. Then we would jump in the car and drive 2.5 hours to Aspen for night training. After the X Games training had finished late at night, Ben and I drove back to Copper Mountain ready for the next day on the SBX track.

Everyone was really welcoming and supportive at the NorAm. I was in the gates with young girls, who would say things like, "I can't believe I am riding alongside Torah Bright." I was getting a ton of help from riders and coaches. I was loving the support and taking it all in. A lot of people asked me why I was doing three events. I'd just reply, "why not?" Giacomo Kratter, an Italian snowboarder, said to me: "I don't know why you are doing this." I said, "I don't either. But it's really working for me. I am back and enjoying snowboarding more than I ever have."

One evening on the drive back to Copper from Aspen, Ben and I were chatting away. We were discussing what was needed for one of the SBX events the next day when all of a sudden we saw flashing blue and red lights in the side mirrors of the car. Benny must have been speeding. Benny handed his licence to the policeman who said he'd be back shortly. A few moments later the police asked Ben to step out of the vehicle and they handcuffed him. It turned out that Ben had a traffic violation from 2007 that was unpaid.

I followed as Ben was taken to the Glenwood Springs, CO prison. I had to post bail. I was told it would take about an hour to process. I decided to take a little nap in the car while I waited. Just as I closed my eyes, I heard a knock on the window of my car. I looked out and saw a man holding a baby with no blanket. It was a typical Colorado cold night – freezing. I wound the window down a little and asked what was going on. The man told me that the baby wouldn't stop crying asked me if I knew anything about babies. "Well he's cold," I said. "Don't you have a blanket or something you can wrap him in?" The man looked mystified. I got out of the car and took the baby from him. It was freezing, probably minus 20 degrees. He walked me to his car.

He said that his friends were in a domestic dispute, that the police had been called and there was an automatic restraining order placed on them. The poor little guy was cold and hungry. I wrapped him up in a blanket and fed him some of his bottle. I cuddled him and got him to sleep. I transferred him into his car seat and went back to my car to take that nap. I was only in my car for about five minutes when the man came to the car again with the baby. He had woken up again. I got out of the car again, to tend to the baby. I stood out in the cold with the car door open with the heat blowing on the baby, bouncing him to sleep in my arms. "Okay, he's asleep again. If you hold him he will stay asleep," I said. "Na just put him back in his car seat," the man told me. "If I do that you'll have to rock his car seat to keep him asleep," I replied.

The man had no idea what to do with the baby so I decided to sit in his car, hold the baby and keep him asleep. He really liked that idea. I know this sounds dangerous but I didn't have a bad feeling about him, which I know doesn't make the situation unequivocally safe but in that moment I was more worried about the baby than my own safety. An hour and a half passed and there was no sign of the mother, the dad hadn't been released

Getting the goods, sunrise at Thredbo, 2014

Checking the pipe at the 2006 Olympic Games, Torino, Italy

Getting ready to drop in, Dew Tour, 2013

With Mike Wagner and Benny – the dream team, Lake Louise, Canada, 2013

Montafon, Austria, December, 2013

Standing on the top of Rosa Khutor,
Sochi Olympic test event, Febuary,
2013

Using the natural landscape of the
Moroccan mountains on a Roxy
photo shoot, 2008

World Superpipe Championships,
Park City, Utah, 2006

Nippon Open champagne showers,
2006

Heli boarding is not as fun as
everyone says

My shirtless Aussie fan club, 2006 Olympics, Torino, Italy

Family love: Marion (left), Rowena (right), 2006 Olympics

Shredding babes in the debut of slopestyle at the Sochi 2014 Olympic Games

With Sarah Burke at the Women's Sports Foundation after party

Water on the rocks while out dancing with Cassie Michelin, Gold Coast, Queensland, 2004

Making music with Scotty in New Zealand, 2012.

Image right: Getting into the spirit of movember with Alicia Wade

80s night with Erin Comstock and Hana Beaman

Cowgirls – with Abish on the Gold Coast, Queensland

With Sarah Burke enjoying our favorite cupcakes in a NYC
hotel room, 2009

At a fancy dinner with
Stine Brunkjildas in
Madrid, Spain on a Roxy
PR tour, 2007

ESPY's red carpet
with Sarah Burke,
2007

ESPY with sister
Rowena, 2007

NYC Subway Red Dress fashion show, Febuary 2013

With Ben at the fashion show, 2013

With shred babes, Left to right: Chanel Stadics, Steph, Sarah Burke,
Elena Height and Kirsty Leskinen

At the World Superpipe Championships, Park City, Utah, 2006

X Games with the younger generation of shredders, 2006

Spring shredding with Scotty and Benny, New Zealand, 2013

NAME: SCOTTY JAMES AND TORAH BRIGHT
TEAM: AUSTRALIA
SPORT: SNOWBOARD

JAAS FULLER BRIGHTO
R GBR AUS
OWBOARDDDDERSS

With Scotty James, Kjersti
Buaas and Aimee Fuller, in the
Sochi Olympic village, 2014

SOCHI 2014 OLYMPIAN
www.olympic.org/hub
#olympichub

After receiving my Order of Australia Medal, with my parents and
brother Robin, May 2011

Tummy time with Rowena's baby Syd, 2008

Looking forward to the future on and off my board

from prison, and neither had Ben.

I asked him, "What would the mother think if she came back and a random woman was holding her baby?"

"This baby would be dead if it wasn't for you," he said.

It felt a little like David Lynch had decided to direct my life but I hung in there. A few people had been let out and I was looking for Ben. When I spotted him, I opened the car door and got out with the baby in my arms and yelled to him. "Benny. Over here." Ben walked over to me with a concerned look on his face. I got out of the car and put the baby back in its car seat. I asked if the man would hold the baby so he would stay asleep. He said "No, just put him in his car seat." I don't know what happened to the man or the baby but yet again, my life felt terribly symbolic. I was figuratively and literally left holding the baby that night.

By the time we were on the road again it was 12.30 am and we still had a 40-minute drive. When we finally made it home I fell into bed fully clothed. The next day was the first SBX event. I made it through the time trial and into the round. I scored a place in the finals but due to a collision with another rider over a feature I had to settle for fourth. The next day I placed 2nd. I had enough points to attend the Blue Mountain World Cup in Canada. The SBX quest could continue.

2012–2013 Season

4th Place – Dew Tour Breckenridge, Superpipe – 2012

9th Place – FIS World Cup 12/13, Superpipe – 2012

4th Place – Winter X Games Tignes, Superpipe – 2012

7th Place – Winter Games Aspen, Superpipe – 2012

7th Place – FIS World Cup 12/13, Superpipe – 2013

4th Place – X Games Aspen, Superpipe – 2013

RUN FOURTEEN

3rd Place – FIS World Cup Stoneham, Slopestyle – 2013

1st Place – US Snowboarding Copper Mountain Grand Prix, Superpipe – 2013

RUN FIFTEEN

'One thing you can give and still keep is your word.'
– Unknown

Time was not on my side. I had just over 12 months to get my SBX points up if I was to achieve my goal of competing in three Winter Olympic snowboarding events. Blue Mountain in Ontario Canada was the first SBX World Cup event I could do and the first event that would count towards my Olympic qualification.

To be competitive in the SBX, we knew that I would need different snowboards. My Roxy Bright Edition line is designed for freestyle riding. The SBX boards are a different construction. They're designed to go as fast as possible. At NorAm I'd ridden with my half pipe boards and I turned up at Blue Mountain with my freestyle snowboards again. I wanted to ride a world cup course before I made up my mind and invested in boards. It was highly possible this whole three-event thing was a fantasy I'd soon abandon. I know I was laughed at. People were saying that I thought I was "so good I could just turn up on anything and win." This was anything but my reality. I knew I would not be competitive on the style of board I was riding, but I needed the experience to understand more about what it was going to take. I was willing to risk being laughed at while I did what

I had to. I didn't qualify for the finals, but I didn't come last either. I could see what I needed to do and how the technique for riding the features was different. It is almost completely opposite to the way I ride the park and pipe. It was going to take some time to develop the proper techniques.

The next event was the World Cup at the Olympic venue in Sochi, Russia in February 2013. This event is a test event for the Olympics. The officials and the athletes are able to experience the venues and get a feel for the surroundings. Benny had organized two SBX-specific snowboards for me to try while I was in Russia. I planned to do three test events however the slopestyle was cancelled due to lack of snow. The cancellation didn't matter so much, it freed up some time for me to test the new SBX boards.

The boards were really fun to ride at high speed. The problem for me was that when I was hitting jumps I felt like I was in the back seat and kept landing on my tail. That's not the way I usually ride jumps so I was very confused. I really had to manhandle the board to get it to do what I wanted. Snowboard cross boards are bigger with different side cuts. They are designed to go fast while half pipe boards are designed for flow, pop and have a playful power. There was a lot to get my head around. I am used to the mantra: 'the more air the better' but in SBX, the less air you get, the quicker you're able to get back to the snow, which means the faster you are. Also, having to memorize the courses was new to me. Making sure the boards have the right structure and wax for snow conditions has always been important in the freestyle realm but it is even more important in speed and timed events. We knew this from our ski racing days and, of course, from Rowena.

When the idea of doing SBX was actually set in motion, Ben and I reached out to Mike Wagner for his advice. Mike was the guy who made my boards 'too fast' at the 2010 Olympics. We were asking him to point us in the right direction and it was a huge surprise and absolute honour when he said that he wanted to help us on the journey. Mike is a very busy man. He did a lot of juggling with his schedule to make time to be with us. The first events he was planning to join us were at Arosa and Veysonnaz in Switzerland in just four weeks' time.

A lot of riders were unhappy when the test event for slopestyle in Sochi was cancelled. We were also disgruntled at the condition of the half pipe. Many competitors, especially the US riders, voiced their concerns and wanted the builders replaced. They were the same builders we had in Vancouver. Everyone wanted Snow Park Technologies (SPT) to come in and build the half pipe for the games. SPT build the parks and pipes on the professional tour and they are very good at what they do. They are passionate and work until it is right and to the standard we need as professional riders. I was told that SPT did place a bid for the building of the slope and pipe, but they did not get the contract.

Everyone was frustrated. The pipe was inconsistent and lot of good riders fell because it was too hard to manage. I fell on both runs in the final of the half pipe test event. Luckily I wasn't relying on points for my Olympic qualification. After the half pipe event there was the SBX to get through. This would be the first time that I would ride an SBX-specific board on a track. I was able to get some runs on the mountain and feel out the boards, see how they turned and how they felt at speed. They are great fun to arc a turn, and I was reminded again of my night boarding days with Adam, making trenches with every railed turn. This SBX test event was one I wanted to just experience. I took in all the advice I'd been so generously offered by the snowboarding community and put it into action on the track. I had a friend helping me with my 'wax teching' at the event, Luke Byers.

RUN FIFTEEN

During that winter I had good days and bad days. Sometimes I would wake up pumped; other days I was emotionally wrecked. These fluctuations had an uncanny correlation to the timing of the updates I'd periodically receive from my divorce lawyer. I needed a break. I needed to recharge. Ben and I flew from Zurich to Dubai for four days to soak up the sun while my mind worked overtime on all sorts of things. Mum had introduced me to a type of energy therapy that works on every level. It's called lifeline technique. I had a session over Skype to help me release the burdens of my personal life and to reconnect to my true essence and self and not be defined by the projections of others. After the session, I returned to Benny on the beach. "Hey" I said as I sat down. "Wow, you look different," he said. "Really? Yeah, I feel different." I went on to explain that I felt like layers and layers had just fallen off of me.

Ben and I flew back to Zurich and picked up our luggage from our friend Vernon's house. He lent us his car while he was off on a snowboard trip taking photographs. We loaded it up and took off to Laax, Switzerland for a week of shredding. In Laax I was able to ride some jumps and get some hours on the SBX boards. I was riding the jumps one afternoon and I came up short on the landing. As I compressed on the knuckle of the jump, I kneed my chin and chipped a few of my bottom teeth. One was bad enough that I needed to see a dentist. I was angry with myself that I had ridden without a mouth guard again.

I brushed myself off and we headed to Arosa. Luke was there as my wax tech. Things were going well and it was great to be on another track. I was really getting into SBX by this point and loving my new SBX friends. Australians Belle Brockhoff and Jarryd Hughes were a great support to me. I thought it was extremely gracious that Belle wasn't annoyed at me waltzing into her world. She generously welcomed me and shared her knowledge. I guess what it comes down to is that we all just love our sport, so we're happy to share it (and enjoy it) with anyone who's interested.

After Arosa, Luke, Ben and I drove to Veysonnaz to meet Mike Wagner. He was going to be with us for the next two SBX World Cups. Veysonnaz was somewhat of a breakthrough event for me. The morning of the time trial I woke up feeling off. It was one of those divorce lawyer days. I needed to snap out of my funk quickly as there was no time for me to throw away an event. I had to make it count. When I arrived on the mountain, I went and sat quietly by myself. I used some of the energetic techniques like tapping of the heart chakra to balance me and to put me in the state of mind that I wanted to be in. I realized that it was important for me to stay present for these emotions, but I was not obliged to stay in them. So I stood up and left them behind. I got ready for the time trials. I felt fast in training and I was. I qualified 13th. I was told by the other competitors that it was a great qualification: "If you're in the top 15, you are really racing." For the first time, Ben and I felt like our goal was actually reachable. I had qualified into the next day's events, the rounds. I now had to take on the other competitors on the track. This made me nervous as I didn't have much experience with reacting to other riders but I was excited. I was loving this new challenge. Ben and I talked a lot that night about strategy and who to stay clear of. There are lots of tactics to SBX riding.

As the gate went down we all pulled out of the start. The first few features went well, and on about the third feature a girl went down in front of me on the fastest section of the course. I had a split second to decide what to do. I ended up choosing to sit back. We were going so fast that the sit down turned into a whiplash. I hit my head. I remember the impact but nothing else. Apparently I got up and kept riding. There was an up hill section in the course and I guess I unbuckled one foot and pushed myself up it. I remember a really loud and intense noise in my head and I have a vague memory of buckling my foot back in to continue down the course. I was on auto-pilot. Ben had drilled in to me that I needed to finish the course no matter what because any points I could accumulate were valuable. I continued on down the course, hitting all features. I crossed the finish line and got a result. After the finish I laid down. Jarryd Hughes came up to me and unbuckled my feet from my board and asked if I was okay. Apparently I said "yes". He helped me up and we started walking, except I was walking in zigzags. People raced up to me, grabbed me and sat me down. Once I had sat down, I became emotional and shed some tears. People were asking me "what's wrong" and apparently I answered: "I just realized what a state my life is in." I had moments where my head and eyes were rolling back almost like I was losing consciousness. It was a terrible sign to appear to be okay and then regress. The helicopter was called and I was airlifted off the mountain to the hospital for scans of my brain. I came to in the helicopter but was not aware of what had happened.

The scans came back clear, but yes, I had given myself yet another concussion. This was the worst one I had suffered. I remember Mike and Luke coming to see if I was okay in the hospital. I felt terrible that Mike had come all this way and reorganized his schedule to help me and I was injured again. Mike cared for me like a daughter; he just wanted me to take care of me and help me recover. The next SBXs event was in Sierra Nevada, Spain, which we had tickets for, but we weren't going to go. I had a long recovery ahead. Benny organized a hotel in the town below the mountain for a week. I was on strict orders to rest. I knew the drill now. If Ben had his way, we would have been in a hotel for two weeks before flying back to Utah but I was stubborn and wanted to go back after a week.

It was much more comfortable for me to be home and have my own space.

OWIA (Olympic Winter Institute of Australia) had a connection with a medical group in Ogden, Utah. When I arrived home they looked after me. They arranged treatment in hyperbaric chambers. Which means I lay in a tube breathing 100 percent oxygen in order to aid recovery. This kind of therapy is in its experimental stages but I was happy to be proactive in all ways. Ben drove me the 40-minute journey to these appointments for weeks. It took three months for me to recover, the precious remaining months of the crucial northern winter season. My energy levels were down and I was suffering headaches. I took it easy, slept a lot, and slowly recovered. If any symptoms developed, I would simply rest. I did not plunge into depression in the way I had in the course of the last concussion during my marriage. It reaffirmed that I had made the right decision.

That summer I was deliriously happy. I pottered about at home and caught up with friends and had plenty of adventures with Obi. When I was cleared for flight in August, I flew to Australia. After my first lot of concussions, we placed a material 'unequal' into my helmets. It's a military grade Kevlar material and helps to absorb the impact of a head hit. With this new material in my helmet I felt safe heading home to start riding and training. I spent a lot of time riding in Australia as the parks were amazing. Local park builders, Charles Beckensall and Dougie Graham, spend their northern winters building the parks in Whistler, British Columbia. Because of this, a lot of industry snowboarders were coming to Australia to ride, which was great to see.

We were planning a spring camp in Mount Hutt in October and November, which would have to be privately funded by the athletes themselves. Danny Davis, Queralt Castelet and I fronted the money for the build to start. We invited a fun crew to ride with and prepare for the Olympics. It was just the right mix of athletes at the camp. We finished on November 15 and I flew to Sydney for some pre-Olympic media and jumped on a plane to the US just in time for the northern winter.

Time was running out. I decided to give the SBX quest another crack. Montafon in Austria was the first event of the season in December. I made it through the qualifications and into the rounds, a good start but I still needed better results to get an Olympic qualification. For now I was off to the Dew Tour in Breckenridge, Colorado for the half pipe. It felt great to be back in the half pipe. The pipe at the Dew Tour was manicured beautifully and was such a pleasure to ride. When a pipe is perfect, you can just let your board go and rip it. In the final, I laid down a great first run. I was in first place. When I got to the top Ben asked me what I would like to do for the next run. "I'm not sure, I don't think I can do that run any better than I did, it felt great," I said. Ben was of the same opinion. We tossed out a few ideas and decided that it was best to just do surf slashes down the walls of the pipe. I was told later that as I was slashing, Mick Fanning was surfing his way to 2013 ASP World Tour Champion at the Pipe Masters in Hawaii. It turned out that slash run was in honour of Mick and a victory lap for me. I stayed in first place.

Straight after that event, we were off to Lake Louise in Canada for another SBX world cup FIS event. I had become friends with a bunch of the snowboard cross athletes and even though I did not make finals, I was cheering Jarryd and the other Aussie team on from the sidelines. Jarryd won his first world cup snowboarder cross, aged 18. It was a huge success for him. Ben and I travelled home to Utah where we spent Christmas and celebrated what I called my Golden Birthday. I was turning 27 on the 27th of December. It was beautiful to be back in Salt Lake City connecting with all those who I loved. It was also nice to take my mind off the chance that

I would not make the SBX qualification for the Olympics.

The next event for snowboard cross was in Andorra, at Vallnord-Arcalis, in early January. It's an interesting place. Andorra is a small country in the southern range of the Pyrenees between France and Spain. Importantly for me, this was my last chance to qualify. We had to make the event in time and we had to get a qualifying result. We had troubles with our flights due to bad weather. We had a tight connection and I had a feeling I could not shift. I somehow just knew I needed repack when we arrived in Denver. I picked up my snowboard bag and repacked it into a smaller carry-on bag I bought at the airport. I took my boots, bindings, helmet goggles and outerwear, everything I would need on the hill. Just as I'd worried, no bags arrived in Zurich but as long as Mike arrived with the boards, I had everything with me to be on the hill. Benny and I had a 10-hour drive ahead to Andorra so we grabbed some toothbrushes and underwear from the airport supermarket, got in the car and headed south. Mike was there with the boards. I flooded with relief. I could compete. There were two events in Andorra and I needed an 8th and 9th to secure my Olympic qualification. I came in 8th and 11th. I was satisfied that I was racing and in the top 10. It proved that I could race. I was happy if that was all that came out of this journey. I felt bad about Mike giving so much time to me when I was not really getting the results we wanted. However, it was not quite over yet. The way the Olympic qualifications worked, there was a chance that I could get a last-minute spot if not all the countries reached their full four-place quota. I decided that I would surrender my SBX Olympic fate to the universe. There were 24 possible SBX Olympic spots, with only four allocated to each country. I was 26th on the FIS list, and I needed to be inside the top 24.

Meanwhile, we realized that I was slipping down in the ranks for slopestyle. We had to make last minute plans to get to another slopestyle event. Ben and I flew straight from Andorra to Quebec City. We worked out that if I could get a top 12, I would have enough points to safely stay within the top 30 on the FIS list. I rode through the qualifications and made it through to the semi finals. Ben and I triple-checked to make sure that if I walked away from the event, I would get last place in the semi finals, which would actually be 10th in the whole event. This would still give me the points I needed. The rule book confirmed that I would be given the 10th place if I did not compete. This meant that I was guaranteed an Olympic start in slopestyle. We took off back to Salt Lake to prepare for the Olympics, only two weeks away.

I needed a lot more time on snow, especially for the slopestyle. I had not ridden it enough. Park City Mountain Resort a short distance from Salt Lake has supported me for years and gave me snowmobile rides all day. It meant that I didn't have to waste any time on the lifts and got a lot of work done. I was bruised and sore and was falling a lot but I worked my butt off. I was enjoying pizza one Saturday after training with friends in Provo when my phone buzzed. An email had landed. I had my spot in the SBX at the Olympics. It was a fabulous feeling. It was everything I'd been working for and what I wanted. With a giddy rush I announced to everyone: "I'm a Triple Threat. T3 has just become a reality!"

It was time for Sochi. We left Salt Lake on the first of February. Ben and I had our tiger team sending us off at the airport. Katie Perry's 'Roar' had become my anthem. I whispered the lyrics to myself as I rode and screamed them while dancing with my sister. Perry's Helen-Reddy-inspired reworking of Survivor's iconic Rocky-montage-song was the perfect poem to get me through my own Rocky-esque-montage-triple-event-Olympic-journey-quest. My little nephews wore tiger t-shirts and also gave Ben and I tiger t-shirts for the season. I wore mine under my outerwear at the Olympics. I was going to need my tiger-team-power. Russia wasn't high on my list of places to visit. My experience at the trials a year before had not been great. The facilities were not to a standard that any of us had expected. There were also a lot of reports of terrorism in Russia and I kept being asked if I thought it was safe to go. I had no idea. I only had the same information as everyone else. All I knew for certain was that I was horrified by the archaic homophobic laws and I was so proud of my teammate, Belle Brockhoff, who came out publicly in the lead up to the event. The Olympics, as a celebration of diversity and humanity should be about pride and I was so moved to see how much pride Belle had.

1st Place – Dew Tour Breckenridge, Superpipe – 2013

February 2013 SBX World Cup Blue Mountain, Canada

February 2103 SBX World Cup Sochi, Russia

March 2013 SBX World Cup Arosa, Switzerland

March 2013 SBX World Cup Veysonnaz, Switzerland

March 2013 SBX World Cup Sierra Nevada, Spain

December 2013 SBX World Cup Montafon, Austria

December 2013 SBX World Cup Lake Louise, Canada

RUN SIXTEEN

'The greatest devastation in the history of the world is not war or crime, but that human beings don't live up to their potential.'
– Sterling W. Sill

There was no way my family would be surprising me in Russia. My sister Rowe had just had her third baby, Abi was busy running her hair salon and mum, dad and Robin were happy to support me from home. Ben and I flew to Frankfurt to pick up an Olympic charter flight that would get us straight to Sochi. Sochi is a city nestled along the shore of the Black Sea, east of the Ukraine. From there we would be heading to the mountains into the wilderness of Rosa Khutor Extreme Park in Krasnaya Polyana.

I had a crazy amount of gear. I was travelling with 12 boards. I had four for each event, and each one had been prepped for different snow conditions. Half of my personal bags were full of food as our gastronomic experiences during our previous trip to Russia had not been great. I would absolutely have to keep my nutrition up to manage the three events. I packed sprouted nuts, raw dark chocolate, seaweed snacks as well as protein powders, essential oils, vitamins and minerals.

Scotty James was on the plane, so the three of us planned to hit Sochi together just as we had in Vancouver. Scotty had qualified for Sochi in both half pipe and slopestyle. He was riding really well coming off a 4th at the recent X Games and was now owner of a Crystal Globe, as the FIS 2013–14 World Cup series half pipe winner. When we arrived into Sochi I was relieved to find that all of my bags had arrived. We said hello to the media then hopped on a bus and headed to the Athletes village in Rosa Khutor.

At the first press conference of the Olympics I expressed my (and my fellow riders') concerns about the quality of our facilities. The pipe and slopestyle needed changes and a lot of work. We expected a course similar to the professional circuit and were within our rights to demand it. The Olympics is the largest stage we have to showcase the sport of snowboarding. It was terribly disappointing that the level of build did not allow us to demonstrate what we are all capable of. Snowboarding can be life threatening. That's why it is vitally important that the build is correct. I was shocked when the media around the world lashed back at us, calling us 'whinging athletes'. The challenging courses were our reality. We had to risk our lives riding them. Thankfully changes were made to the slope course, and each day got better as rider input was put into play. The pipe, however, was somewhat of a nightmare, and a few riders were injured during training.

On the first training day for slopestyle, IOC officials were out making sure logos and other paraphernalia met regulations. Along with many others, I had a 'Sarah' sticker on my helmets and boards, in memory of my dear friend and in respect for all the work she had done to put freestyle skiing where it was today: in the Olympics. An IOC official pointed at me and said: "You are not allowed that. You can't wear that." He went on to say it was a political statement and therefore propaganda. I had to remove it. I think Sarah's coach Trennan put it best when he said it was "unbelievable how much Sarah's memory has pulled us all together. Things will never be the same without her, but I can tell you that when we walk into the Sochi Olympic stadium, Sarah is going to be the one leading the team." We were all there to ride for Sarah, sticker or no sticker.

I've always loved to dance, especially with my sisters. Some of my first memories are of dancing on the kitchen bench at home in Cooma to Mariah Carey and Biggie Smalls. Dancing is a pure joy to me; it's expressive, freeing and energising. Throughout my Olympic journey to Sochi, Rowe had been sending me dances via Instagram to songs tailored for the moment. She knew that putting herself out there on the Internet would make me laugh and keep me relaxed. It had become a fun game for us. Sometimes she'd dance so hard that she couldn't move her neck the next day. We had both recorded dances for our other friends on their Olympic journeys while they were trying to qualify. We would sometimes spend an hour just to get a 14-second Instagram bite. The game evolved and during the Olympics, Rowe put a call out for all of my supporters to send me a dance via the hashtag #torahtime. I was overwhelmed by the response. These videos made me smile and laugh so loudly, and gave me so much strength. These dances are some of my fondest memories of the Sochi Olympics.

On the first day of slopestyle training, I took a hard landing and hurt my knee. It became an injury that I had to nurse through the whole games. The US snowboarder Danny Davis (who was also working with Ben) had a physiotherapist with him whom I had worked with on the Dew Tour. Courtney had an incredibly painful technique that released the hamstring. We did it so often to help me stay on the snow that I was black and blue. Every day after riding I had an ice bath in a green wheelie rubbish bin. Then it was heat at night on the injuries.

I was in physiotherapy one evening when I took a phone call from my friend, Alicia. I could not hear her very well. She was crying so much she could barely talk. After about five or six attempts, I finally heard her say, "Neena lost her baby." She was 37 weeks along. We cried together trying to comprehend this devastating news. We talked about how horrible the pain must be. When we hung up, I got in the ice bath. For the first time I lowered myself to my neck in the freezing water. I was emotionally freezing and numb from the news and I wanted my body to feel likewise. While I was in the ice bath, I got a text from Andy, Neena's husband, letting me know the situation. It became real at that moment. I could not control the tears that fell from my eyes. I called Rowena and cried some more with her. I was shivering in a ball on the floor of my room deliberating over whether to call Andy. I did not know what to say to him but eventually I called and told them I loved them.

The next day I tried to get a grip on myself so I could use the day to prepare for slopestyle. I was having a hard time focusing and a harder time being in my body. I was crying on every lift ride. It was a day that I probably should have just surrendered to my emotions and not tried to be so brave. That night was the Olympic opening ceremony and I wanted to write a post that would let them know how deeply I cared. I decided that I was going try to be a strength for them both. Neena and Andy were among the few people with whom I had shared the traumas of my divorce. Their support was always healing and uplifting. They stayed up all night and helped make decisions about my marriage. It deeply distressed me that I couldn't be there for them while they were experiencing such sadness.

The qualifications for slopestyle came and went. I was straight into the final and was happy with my riding. When it came to the finals, my cab 720 was not working. It was Ben's suggestion to step it up to a cab 900. It looked like my body mechanics were better prepared for that. I was unable to land it without a hand drag, which lowered my score. Even so, I was happy to have a new trick to work on and perfect for the next time I rode jumps. I placed seventh that day. Jamie Anderson won. She is one of the best, with such solid style and technical trickery. It is always nice when the best can perform and be rewarded. Enni Rukajärvi of Finland came in second and British rider Jenny Jones was third. I was so proud and so excited to watch all my friends ride.

The men's half pipe competition was the night before the women's. Scotty was the first rider to drop and his low score shocked and confused many athletes, commentators and Scotty himself. He did a fabulous run and the score he should have received would have put him in the semi finals. Danny Davis, who had been through devastating injuries and yet had won X Games just weeks before the Olympics was my pick to take the half pipe win. A group of us were watching the guys' competition in the Aussie house. It was a sad sight. A lot of riders were going down. It was very obvious that the pipe was not up to standard. When the event was over, I stayed just looking at the screen. I could not believe that was it. It was the saddest event I have ever seen. The pipe let those boys down that night.

Finally it was my moment in the half pipe. I qualified straight through to finals, winning my heat. While the pipe was in better condition than it had been for the guys, it was still not in great shape. During the semi finals, I made my way back to the Olympic Village to take a shower and refresh. My nephews Syd and Lyon insisted on sending me a little message before the finals. I was so happy to receive it. Syd, unscripted, earnestly informed me that: "As long as you do your best, you always win. No matter if you get a bronze, silver or gold, last place or tenth, as long as you do your best, you always win." I melted hearing this little speech, as it was completely true, straight from the heart of a six-year-old. Syd had unwittingly paraphrased the Olympic creed that Pierre de Coubertin adopted: 'The most important thing in life is not the triumph, but the fight; the essential thing is not to have won, but to have fought well.' It was strangely tense that night. Usually the mood in the half pipe is much lighter. I prepared for the first of my two runs in the final. Benny said a few words to me and I moved down the drop-in ramp to prepare. As I was doing this, the volunteers on the side of the pipe started to bang their poles together cheering for me. It was really unexpected and sweet, so I smiled, laughed, and blew a kiss to them all. I had to take another moment to collect myself before I dropped in.

I remember my first trick, the McTwist, then air-to-fakie into a stylish cab 720, it all felt so good. Then it was the easiest trick in my run that got me. The front side 540. I fell. It's always nice to put down a clean run on the first so you can up the ante on the second. Now I had to focus on landing the second run. Benny did not seem fazed so I just floated around the top of the pipe doing my thing, staying loose, a little bit of dancing, a little bit of singing with anyone that would goof around with me. I was with Kelly Clark for a minute and she was extremely tense. I gave her a hug, we let go and I told her she needed another hug, I quickly corrected myself, "I mean, I need another hug." We hugged again.

I got ready for my second run. I slipped into position and waited for my smile. I let all the pressure go, and focused on being in the moment. I dropped in and my first McTwist felt really good. I then performed an air-to-fakie into cab 720. Landing, I came down really heavily. My head was between my legs. I was looking at my board and boots and thinking, that's weird, I never see them. It did not hinder my line or speed into the next trick. I held my composure through the front side 540 which got me on the first run, front side alley-oop was next into my final trick, backside alley-oop rodeo. The pipe was inconsistent and I had to muscle out one landing low in the transition. However, I had done my best. The scores took forever to come through. 91.5: I was in second place by .25. Kaitlyn Farrington was in first on 91.75, and Hannah Teter was coming third on 90.50. Kelly Clark was the last rider to come down, so no matter what happened I was taking home either a silver or bronze. I couldn't stop smiling as I watched Kelly finish her run. Kelly bumped Hannah into fourth with a score of 90.75. I had silver. I was beside myself. It felt like gold.

Circe and Ben were by my side within moments. There was a flower ceremony at the venue and then the long media line commenced. Then it was straight into drug testing. The old pee in a bottle in front of a stranger routine, my least favorite thing about FIS. I called Rowena as soon as I could. Back in Utah she had hosted a party so all my friends could watch, dance and cheer me on together. I was so happy to talk to everyone. When I arrived home after the drug test it was about 2 am. I was buzzing and couldn't sleep. I think I managed to kip for a total of about 30 minutes before I was up for an early morning press conference. My schedule was pretty perfect. I had a day off before I was due to commence SBX training which meant even though I was exhausted, I was free for media and celebrations. I was dancing all through those Olympic Games. I could not seem to stop. I even took the dancing onto the podium. I was trying to be respectful of the ceremony, but I could not resist a little shimmy. After the medal ceremony, I was straight into training. The medal party the Australian team were going to throw me would have to wait until after I finished my SBX event.

To qualify for SBX in the Olympics was a true challenge, but it was also the event I had ridden the most in recent months. It was the event I was perhaps most prepared for. But in snowboard cross you never know what can happen. There were riders falling in front of me on every training run. I was not able to make a clean run through the course because of being red flagged. This means you must stop because there is an injured person on the course. I had a slow first qualifying run. My second run was much faster and qualified me in a decent position. During the first round, I was up against five others, including my Australian teammate, Belle Brockhoff. I fell behind on a few of the first features by not making big enough moves on them, I got too much air. But I was working hard to catch up. I overtook one girl on a flat section and Belle was in front on me. I was gaining on her. We were coming into the second last corner and I was coming in hot. I had to make a choice. I either had to try to overtake her or get out of her way. If I tried to overtake her, I risked taking both of us out. I chose to get out of her way. I was happy to look up and see Belle riding off. She advanced through to the next rounds and ended up eighth. My Sochi Olympic journey was over. T3 accomplished. With my gold in Vancouver and my silver in Sochi, I am now Australia's most successful female winter Olympian. For now. I look forward to watching the younger generation of shredders surpass what I've done.

2014

8th and 11th Place – SBX World Cup x 2 Vallnord-Arcalis, Andorra
– January 2014

10th Place – Snowboard Jamboree, Slopestyle, Quebec City –
January 2014

Silver Medal – Sochi Winter Olympics, Half pipe

7th Place – Sochi Winter Olympics, Slopestyle

18th Place – Sochi Winter Olympics, Boardercross

RUN SEVENTEEN

'In the end, we'll all become stories.'
– Margaret Atwood

What does the future hold? For now I am happily snowboarding on. I'll figure out my path as I shred my way down the mountain of life. I'm not afraid to turn, to try new things, to explore all the possibilities the backcountry has to offer. I truly believe it takes courage to claim your true purpose. To quiet the outside voices and just finally be you. I have felt my life either expand or shrink in direct proportion to my courage. I chose to keep fighting. Just as Katy Perry sings in my morale boosting favorite tune, 'I went from zero to my own hero.' I've faced my doubts and demons and I've won. I am a champion. I really don't mean that in the elite athlete sense. I'm much more interested in the way I've chosen to live and the way that makes me a champion. C.S. Lewis wrote that 'Courage is not simply one of the virtues, but the form of every virtue at the testing point.' Courage at this point in my journey is about being willing and able to live in the power and peace of infinite love and gratitude.

I learned from my Vancouver experience that going straight on to compete in other events directly after the Olympics is not a good idea for me. This time, after Sochi, I wanted to relish in my triumphs. I wanted to come home and celebrate. I wanted to write this book. 2014 has been about reflection and enjoying myself. I've kept my usual frenetic pace but this year has been about friends, family, celebration and adventures. I'm taking the time to find out who I am when I'm not shredding. Not to say I haven't been shredding. I totally have.

2014 has brought me lots of amazing experiences. I've spent time in Melbourne competing in the Formula One Grand Prix Celebrity Challenge. This was a dream come true as I'm more than a little fond of fast cars. It was such an amazing experience to be taught how to drive (fast) by Mark Skaife and Daniel Gaunt. Then I headed back to Salt Lake to collect my nephew Syd and fly to LA. My nieces, Janaya and Belle, were visiting the US with their mum so Syd and I met them at Disneyland. I was aunty mummy to Syd for a week as we frolicked around amusement parks hyped up on way too much sugar.

After Disneyland we went to Santa Monica and strolled the quirky Venice Boulevard. Syd says it was one of the best times of his life. Next stop was Sydney for the royal reception at the Opera House with William and Kate, Their Royal Highnesses, The Duke and Duchess of Cambridge. It was a lovely time. It was pleasantly informal and I was thoroughly taken with their graciousness.

Shortly after that I flew to Nicaragua with a rad group of friends for my annual surfing fix. Twelve of us rented a house and we ate well, slept well and surfed well. It was good to connect with my colleagues off the mountain and away from the competitive arena. I also managed to squeeze in a trip to the continent with Rowena. A good friend of hers, the British ski racer, Chemmy Alcott was getting married in London and I had some business in Biarritz, France for my Roxy Bright Edition, so we decided a quick trip to France, and Spain together fitted in well. Next I was off to

Maui to visit the great Julia Mancuso. We had a wonderful time exploring the island, free diving, mountain biking and surfing.

From there I flew back to Salt Lake City, grabbed my bags and was excitedly Australia bound. My youngest sister Abi was due with her first child. I arrived back in Cooma just in time to help she and Max through a long labour. I was also coming home as the new Thredbo ambassador. The winter conditions were the best in 10 years. I could not wait to get shredding and start a creative campaign to share snow fun in Australia.

As you've probably gathered reading this memoir, I'm pretty fond of my childhood texts (and of my childhood). It is these stories that imbued me with my courage, hope, dreams imagination and a sense of fun – none more so than *Mary Poppins*. I can't deny I have had many miracles along the way and some good wind in my sails, but you don't need to buy a kite just fly one, with your family. You just need a dream, and (with your fist holding tight) to hang onto it. Work hard, and pretty soon you'll be 'soaring up through the atmosphere'. And so, I want to impress that 'with tuppence for paper and string' you can indeed 'build your own set of wings'.

Each and every human has an incredible story and journey. This is mine. I hope that my story inspires you to make the most of possibilities and to grab them when they come along. I've learned that if you keep showing up, anything is possible. I've learned that you need to enjoy yourself and listen to yourself when you're not. I've learned that life is about friends and family, and friends who are family. If there's any wisdom I can offer you it's: go outside on powder days and don't be afraid to turn.

REFERENCES

Non-fiction

Allen, C. Kay, *The Ways and Power of Love*, 1993.

Aristotle, *Nicomachean Ethics*, 350 BCE, translated by W. D. Ross.

Clarke, Arthur C., *Report on Planet Three*, 1982.

Curie, Marie in: *Nineteenth Century Science: A selection of original texts*, edited by A.S. Weber, 2000.

Dowrick, Stephanie, *Forgiveness and Other Acts of Love: Finding true value in your life*, Allen & Unwin, 2010

Durant, Will, *The Story of Philosophy: The Lives and Opinions of the World's Greatest Philosophers from Plato to John Dewey*, 1926.

Holmes Sr, Oliver Wendell, *The Entire Works of Sr Oliver Wendell Holmes*, 1858.

Jemison, Dr Mae C., in: *Astronauts*, by Sheila Wyborny, 2001.

Manoranjan, Kumar (ed.), *Dictionary of Quotations*, 2008.

Stanhope, Philip Dormer, Earl of Chesterfield, *Letters to his son, Philip Stanhope*, 1774.

Steinem, Gloria in: *Defending our Dreams: Global feminist voices for a new generation*, edited by Shamillah Wilson, Anasuya Sengupta & Kristy Evans, 1988.

Walker, Alice in: *The Best Liberal Quotes Ever: Why the Left is Right*, by William P. Martin, 2004.

REFERENCES

Fiction

Atwood, Margaret, *Cat's Eye*, 1988.

Atwood, Margaret, *Moral Disorder*, 2006.

Barton, Bruce, *The Man Nobody Knows*, 1925.

Baum, L. Frank, *The Wonderful Wizard of Oz*, 1900.

De Saint-Exupéry, Antoine, *The Little Prince*, 1943.

Lewis, C.S., *The Screwtape Letters*, 1942.

Poetry

Dickinson, Emily, (1830–86), *Part One: Life XCVII,* (*Complete Poems*, 1924).

Waldo Emerson, Ralph, (1803–1882), *Ode*, 1857.

Rossetti, Christina, (1830–1894), *Day-Dreams*, in *Christina Rossetti: Selected Poems*, selected by Jan Marsh, 2010.

Plays

Wilde, Oscar, *Lady Windermere's Fan*, 1892.

Film

Psycho Beach Party, Dir. Robert Lee King, 2000.

When Harry Met Sally, Dir. Rob Reiner, 1989.

TB7 North of Heaven, Standard Films, 1997.

Mary Poppins, Dir. Robert Stevenson, 1964.

Music

Perry, Katy, 'Roar', *Prism*, Capitol Records/Universal, 2013.

REFERENCES

Web

de Coubertin, Pierre, as quoted in: <http://www.olympic.org/documents/reports/en/en_report_1303.pdf > accessed: 30th September 2014.

First published in 2015 by New Holland Publishers Pty Ltd
London • Sydney • Auckland

The Chandlery Unit 9 50 Westminster Bridge Road London SE1 7QY United Kingdom
1/66 Gibbes Street Chatswood NSW 2067 Australia
218 Lake Road Northcote Auckland New Zealand

www.newhollandpublishers.com

Photo Credits
Matt Georges for front and back cover images
Thredbo Alpine Resort for images of Torah at Thredbo, 2014, in 2nd picture section:
Photography by Steve Cuff

A record of this book is held at the British Library and the National Library of Australia.

ISBN 9781742576015

Managing Director: Fiona Schultz
Publisher: Diane Ward
Project Editor: Susie Stevens
Designer: Andrew Quinlan
Production Director: Olga Dementiev
Printer: Ligare Book Printers, Sydney, New South Wales

10 9 8 7 6 5 4 3 2 1

Keep up with New Holland Publishers on Facebook
www.facebook.com/NewHollandPublishers

US $19.99
UK £14.99